D1135627

THE
CHESAPEAKE BAY
Crabbiest
COOKBOOK

WHITEY SCHMIDT

*"A crab provides little food, so
he is not easy to eat. But the
little he does offer is the best
food under the sky. To eat crab
you must work, which makes
you appreciate him more.
He is the blessing, the
remembrance. And no man or
woman ever ate enough."*

An excerpt from Chesapeake *by James Michener.*
Copyright 1978, Random House, Inc.

Printed in the
United States of America

First Printing, Year 2000

ISBN 0-9613008-5-X

Library of Congress Catalog Number 99-96587

© 2000 by Marian Hartnett Press
Box 88, Crisfield, Maryland 21817

All rights reserved.

No part of this book may be reproduced in any manner whatsoever
without written permission except in the case of brief quotations
embodied in critical articles and reviews.

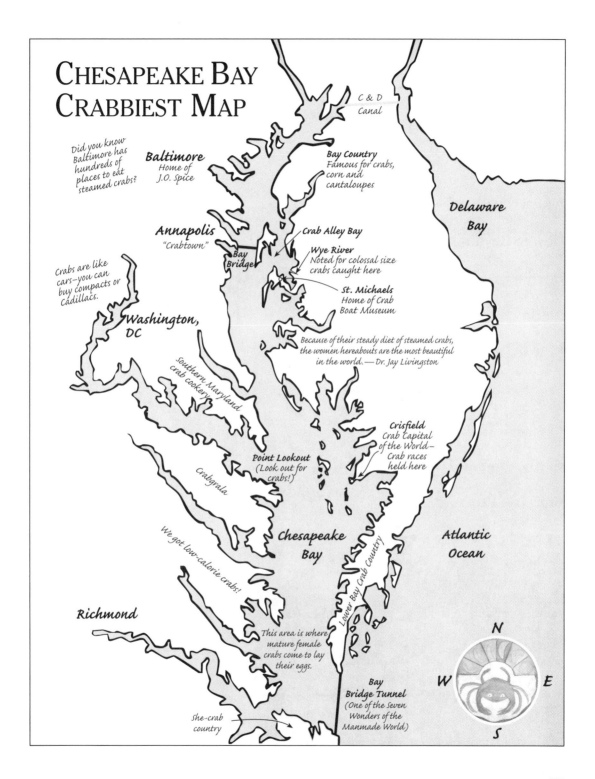

CHESAPEAKE BAY CRABBIEST MAP

Did you know Baltimore has hundreds of places to eat steamed crabs?

Baltimore
Home of J.O. Spice

C & D Canal

Bay Country
Famous for crabs, corn and cantaloupes

Delaware Bay

Annapolis
"Crabtown"

Crab Alley Bay

Wye River
Noted for colossal size crabs caught here

Bay Bridge

Crabs are like cars—you can buy compacts or Cadillacs.

St. Michaels
Home of Crab Boat Museum

Washington, DC

Because of their steady diet of steamed crabs, the women hereabouts are the most beautiful in the world. — Dr. Jay Livingston

Southern Maryland crab cookery

Crisfield
Crab Capital of the World— Crab races held here

Point Lookout
(Look out for crabs!)

Crabgrala

Chesapeake Bay

Atlantic Ocean

We got low-calorie crabs!

Lower Bay Crab Country

Richmond

This area is where mature female crabs come to lay their eggs.

Bay Bridge Tunnel
(One of the Seven Wonders of the Manmade World)

she-crab country

N
W   E
S

CONTENTS

EDITOR'S NOTES

- The recipes in this book are not grouped into chapters by type, but I have included an easy-to-use Index (page 231) that groups the recipes by type so you can quickly find your favorites.

- In the Bay area, we steam our crabs and we're proud of it! If you steam and pick your own crab-meat when preparing the dishes in this book, your results will benefit greatly. The key to the success of a recipe is in the quality of the ingredients you choose.

- The blue crab is the major culinary influence on Chesapeake regional fare—a key element in the cooking and eating lives of Chesapeake Bay residents. This book is a tribute to the blue crab and the people of the Chesapeake Bay area. I hope you'll enjoy cooking and eating these delicious crab dishes as much as we do.

  Whitey Schmidt

INTRODUCTION

The blue crab is the love of my life. I was born on the banks of the Chesapeake Bay, the region this flavorful creature also calls home, and after traveling the world, I can say that the Chesapeake Bay crab is by far the best crab there is. I've talked to other well-traveled crab lovers, and they agree.

Unlike other crab varieties, which are boiled, we steam blue crabs here. The distinctive flavor produced by steaming means that even the smallest crab will have pizzazz. Steaming and eating blue crabs is a ritual, a way of life, for me and all of the others who live in the Chesapeake Bay region or come here in search of that wonderful experience.

That's why I decided to devote this, my eighth book and third cookbook, exclusively to recipes for the blue crab. You'll find recipes here for main dishes, appetizers, soups, crab cakes, and even a crab cheesecake—but don't eat it for dessert! Most of the recipes are ones I created in my "Crab Lab"—my kitchen—using herbs and vegetables from my own garden. Other recipes came from friends, family, restaurant chefs, and winners of the crab-cooking contests I'm frequently asked to judge. All of them have passed my taste test, and most have also been tried on my friends when they dropped by the Crab Lab.

Some of the recipes have interesting stories behind them. Stewed Jimmie's Crab (page 177), for instance, comes from Smith Island, an isle in the middle of the Chesapeake Bay discovered by Captain John Smith of Pocahontas fame, and has been passed down for generations. And my own creation, Crusty Crustacean Crab Bread (page 89), resulted from trying to come up with a roll light enough to properly handle a crab cake. I was kneading the dough, which I soon realized was too heavy, and before I knew it I had shaped it into a crab with legs and claws. I added raisins for eyes and lemon strips for antennae.

This is a book that celebrates not only blue crabs, but the blue crab culture as well. I've written about the life of the crabbers—the watermen who fish for the crabs, setting out each day at 5:00 a.m. And I've included photos I've taken for the past 20 years, all over the Chesapeake Bay, of crab images on everything from police uniform emblems to taxicabs to restaurant signs.

It gives me great pleasure to share my love of crabs with you. Enjoy!

A CHESAPEAKE CRABBER'S DICTIONARY

Buckram—a crab whose shell has not quite hardened

Bushel basket—a place to put crabs and a place to sit when the crabs ain't running

Buster—a molting crab whose shell has split

Channeler—a large, mature male crab (also **jimmie**)

Chicken necker—a weekend or amateur crabber

Crab capital—Crisfield, Maryland

Crab factory—a building housing crab pickers

Crab feast—a traditional gathering much like clam bakes in New England. It's a celebration with steamed crabs piled high and beer flowing freely. Some excellent side dishes are corn on the cob and sliced tomatoes. A crab feast can also mean a restaurant that features all-you-can-eat for a set price.

Crab float—a wooden pen for crab storage; about four feet by twelve feet; used to hold "green" crabs until their molting period

Crab knife—a knife used to pick crabs. Manufactured by Carvel Hall, Crisfield, Maryland.

Crab mustard—the yellow fat of the crab, prized by many and discarded by others. Like garlic, you either love it or hate it. I use it in my crab cakes.

Crab pot—a wire mesh cage, 24 x 24 x 21 inches, with a funnel and buoy for catching crabs. The center trap is baited with fish to entice the crab inside, but once caught he can't get out.

Crab scrape—a lightweight dredge with a toothless bottom bar and a long bag made of twine. It is used to rake through the grass to strain out peelers and soft-shell crabs.

Crab seasoning—a Chesapeake seafood concoction used to season crabs as they steam—a must-have ingredient that can be found in any Chesapeake Bay kitchen, where its distinctive aroma scents the air. We call it "summer's perfume." Look for brands like J.O. Spice, Old Bay and Wye River.

Crab shanty—a building where crabs are taken to be packed for shipment to market, usually at the water's edge

Crabtown—a nickname for Annapolis, Maryland

Crisfield lawn furniture—crab pots that have been pulled from the water and are in need of repair

Dead men's fingers—a crab's gills or lungs (also called **devil's fingers**)

Doubler—a male crab carrying a female for mating (also **buck and rider**)

Dredge—similar to a crab scrape with teeth on the bottom bar. For "wintertime" harvesting of crabs buried in the mud.

Green crab—one of the stages a crab goes through prior to becoming a soft-shell crab. A green crab can also be a live hard crab.

Hard crab—a mature crab between molts

J.O. Spice—a seasoning used by crab houses to spice up their crabs for customers who like them that way

Keeper—a legal-size catch—"That one's a keeper."

Molt—the shedding of a hard shell crab

Number ones—the largest crabs. Remember, the bigger the crab, the bigger the price!

Old Bay seasoning—a spice blend found in the home pantry

Paper shell—a crab whose shell is beginning to harden after molting

Peeler—a crab about to shed

Sally—an immature female crab

Scrape—a dredge or toothed rake pulled over the bay bottom for oysters, clams or crabs

She crab—mature female crab

Slabs—very large soft crabs (also whales)

'S not—'s not a hard crab and 's not a peeler

Soft crab sandwich—one of life's greatest pleasures

Soft-shell crab—crab that has just molted whose shell has not hardened

Sook or Sooky—a mature female crab

Sponge crab—female carrying egg mass

Tinker bells—crab boots worn by watermen. Sometimes they're called Crisfield prom shoes.

Trotline—A method of catching crabs using long baited lines that are buoyed and anchored at each end and rest on river and creek bottoms. The crabber scoops up the unsuspecting crab with a net while the crab eats the bait. Crabs caught on trotlines taste better than those caught by potting or dredging.

LIFE OF THE BLUE CRAB

Blue crabs are found in abundance along the eastern seaboard but prefer waters that range from ocean saltiness to fresh—thus the Chesapeake Bay provides ideal conditions. Life begins in the Lower Bay, where female or "sponge" crabs deposit their eggs between the first of June and the end of August. The baby crabs look very unlike the mature crab and more like a swimming question mark. This "zoea" sheds its shell several times, and when it begins to resemble the adult, it is called a "megalops."

Typically, crabs hatch in late June, pass through the larvae stage by August, and start to move up the Bay during early fall or until cold weather halts their migration. In the spring, their journey is resumed and full maturity is reached when they are twelve to fourteen months old.

In order to increase its size, a crab must molt (shed its outer skeleton). As it approaches a molt, it is called a "peeler." As it actually sheds its old shell it becomes a "soft" crab. It is then velvety in texture and roughly a third again as large as the discarded shell.

During their struggle for existence, crabs frequently lose legs and claws. Within a week of such loss, a new appendage begins to form, but it takes at least two moltings to fully restore the limb.

For some reason, the crab population is very variable and a plentiful season may be followed by a lean one.

HOW TO BUY CRABMEAT

Crabmeat varies in quality and price depending on what part of the crab it comes from. Here are some guidelines for choosing the right type of crabmeat for your recipe:

Jumbo lump: The best and most expensive crabmeat, consisting of whole lumps of white meat from the body of the crab with absolutely no shell or cartilage. Use it in recipes where appearance is important.

Backfin: Large pieces of lump and some broken body meat. It costs less than jumbo lump but tastes as good. It's excellent for casseroles and baked dishes.

Special: "Special" meat is from the entire body of the crab. The pieces are smaller and you'll find more shell.

Claw: Claw meat is darker and sweeter than body meat. Use it in soups or to stretch crab cakes.

Cocktail claws: The last segment of the claw with all shell removed except for the tip, which may serve as a handle for dipping into cocktail sauce.

HOW TO EAT A CRAB

1.

Pry off apron flap on underside
with thumb or knife and lay aside.

2.

Turn the crab over and lift off the top shell
and lay aside. Pull off the claws.

3.

Scrape off the feathery gills—
nobody eats these.

4.

Cut the crab in half and
pull off the legs.

5.

Pick out the meat.

6.

You can eat the claws now
or wait till later, but remember—
Don't smash 'em,
just crack 'em.

PUTTING THE BITE ON SOFT-SHELL CRABS

Soft-shell crabs are an east coast tradition. Out west, the crab is not harvested in its soft stage. The soft crab industry began during the 1870s in Crisfield, Maryland, and today, the soft-shell crab represents a major Chesapeake Bay commercial effort.

The delectable soft-shell crab must be caught right after it has molted. If left in the water, its shell will begin to harden in about two hours. Soft-shell crabs are available from late spring to early fall, with May through August the most productive months.

As the availability of crabs increases during the summer, prices drop. You may wish to purchase a quantity of soft-shells when the price is low and keep them for future use. Clean and wrap them individually before storing them in the freezer. This can easily be accomplished by wrapping the cleaned crab with its legs folded under its body.

Some methods for preparing soft-shells are baking, sautéeing, deep fat frying or pan frying. Other ways of cooking will give equally tasty results. Soft-shell crab sandwiches are one of life's greatest pleasures.

Soft-shell crabs are marketed in the following manner and are sold live, fresh dressed or frozen.

Medium. . . . . 2.5 to 4.0 inches

Hotel . . . . 4.0 to 4.5 inches

Prime . . . . 4.5 to 5.0 inches

Jumbo. . . . . 5.0 to 5.5 inches

Whale . . . . over 5.5 inches

HOW TO DRESS A SOFT-SHELL CRAB

1.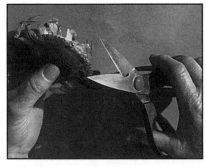

Hold a crab in one hand and snip off the eyes and mouth with scissors. Squeeze out the innards through the opening.

2.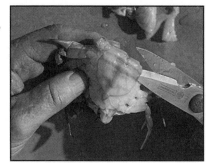

Turn the crab over and snip away the turned apron.

3.

Turn the crab over again and, with your fingers, lift up one pointed corner of the crab's outer shell and snip out and discard the gill.

4.

Repeat the process on the other side, removing the other gill. The crab is now ready to be cooked.

HOW TO SELECT SOFT-SHELL CRABS

The first rule is, get to know your fishmonger. Insist on live crabs—"If it ain't kicking, it ain't cooking" is my motto. Take a crab with little bubbles streaming from its mouth. If they're on ice, have the seller run his hand along the crabs—then choose ones that move. If you can touch them yourself, run your finger along the front points to make sure they're still supple. Avoid "paper-shells"—the softer the crab the better. The smaller crabs, called "mediums," are usually among the sweetest and most tender.

ACKNOWLEDGMENTS

This cookbook has been made possible through the efforts of the following groups and individuals.

John T. Handy Co.

Traugott Schmidt

TAB Distributing Co.

Sue Knopf, Graffolio

Robin Quinn

Mike Dirham

Denise McDonald, cover design

Bill and Gracie Schmidt

Talbot Kitchens

Linton Seafoods

Southern Connection Seafood

Buster Nelson

SELECTED PHOTOGRAPH CREDITS

Vince Lupo, 5, 7, 39, 51, 54, 58, 59, 88, 150, 157, and color insert photos

Marion E. Warren, 180

Noel Schwab, 121, 142, back cover

Bryan Hatchett, 179, 196

Melissa G. Dole, Maryland Watermen's Association, 165, 175, 176, 177, 178

JoAnn Dashiell, 187, 203

Susan Glaser, 80

ILLUSTRATIONS

Margaret Scott, 99, 105

C. Lowry, 112

CRAB LAB TASTE TESTERS

All of the recipes in this book have been tested at least once—some many times. A special thanks goes to these Crab Lab Taste Testers, who have spent countless hours testing and tasting recipes and commenting on flavor and appearance. Thank you all for your enthusiasm for crab cookery. As I always say, "It's a tough job, but someone has to do it."

David Holland

Nancy Holland

Bill Schmidt

Gracie Schmidt

Matt Schmidt

Dean Gore

Tom Vernon

Sue Schryer

Jay Livingston

Melissa Livingston

Eddie Doyle

Raymond McAlwee

Damien Heaney

Joseph Heaney

Mary Heaney

Bridgeen Heaney

Pat Piper

Bryan Hatchett

Vince Lupo

Joe Heurich

Sherry Heurich

Richard Collins

Jimmy Sita

Margie Sita

Bo Herrman

Peggy Fenton

Pat Abate

Jim Abate

Shirley Kenna

Ray Durham

Joyce Durham

Raymond Durham

Jack Sherwood

Betty Sherwood

Camille Durham

Caryn Glenn

Sydney Glenn

Sabrina Donovan

T. L. "Buddy" Schmidt

Kim Schmidt

Kristi Schmidt

Teresa Evans

Traugott Schmidt

Alicia Pritchard

Heather Elgin

Barb Kuebler

Dan Kuebler

Ron White

Briggs White

Linda Leist

Tom Hunter

Burt Elder

Cindy Elder

Susan A. Wills

Carol Hammond

Bob Hammond

Susan Glaser

The gang at Seaside Country Store, Fenwick Island, Delaware

CRAB LAB PANTRY

The Chesapeake Bay region has distinctive ingredients, spices, herbs, seasonings that are used in certain ways or combinations that give "Chesapeake Cuisine" its unique characteristics. Here are a few of my favorites:

Old Bay seasoning—Old Bay is a blend of herbs and spices that is used around Bay Country kitchens. The distinctive aroma of this seasoning scents the air on many a humid day. We call it "Summer's Perfume."

J.O. Spice—People ask me all the time about the secret to Chesapeake Bay cooking. The secret is in the seasonings. Seasoning doesn't mean it's hot and spicy, but that it's a perfect balance of spices and herbs in just the right proportions to complement the crab dish that it's used in. J.O. Spice is used in about eighty percent of the crab houses that cater to Chesapeake blue crabs.

Tabasco Sauce—Tabasco is an extremely hot spicy sauce made from red peppers. Tabasco is used as a condiment and for enlivening a number of crab dishes.

Worcestershire Sauce (*woos*-ter-sheer)—A thin, dark, rather piquant sauce used to season crab cakes and crab imperial. It's also an essential ingredient in the popular Bloody Mary cocktail. Worcestershire's formula usually includes garlic, soy sauce, onions, molasses, lime, anchovies, vinegar and various seasonings. It's widely available throughout the United States.

Beer—Beer and crabs go together just like salt goes with French fries. Locals insist on using flat beer when steaming crabs. To flatten beer, simply pour a bottle into a measuring cup and sprinkle with a little salt. It'll go flatter than a pancake in about an hour. Of course, beer is also the time-honored companion drink to serve with steamed crabs—or any other seafood, for that matter.

CHAPTER 1
Sign of the Crab

SOFT-SHELL CRABS GRILLED IN SOY SAUCE

Cooking outdoors over the last fifty years has become a way of life around the Chesapeake. No longer is it just burgers, ribs and chicken. You'll find that these grilled soft-shell crabs are some of the best you've ever had. Try them tonight!

¼	cup soy sauce
1½	cups white wine
⅓	cup olive oil
6	drops hot pepper sauce
4	cloves fresh garlic, chopped
4	soft-shell crabs

In a shallow baking dish mix soy sauce, white wine, olive oil, hot pepper sauce and chopped garlic. Add soft crabs and cover. Marinate for 2 hours. Wait for the coals to stop flaming in the grill, and place crabs on the rack. Turn a few times, basting frequently. Soft crabs are cooked when firm and slightly crisp.

Serves 2.

In order for a hard-shell crab to grow, it must first molt or shed its old shell. When it molts it is in the soft state that is commonly recognized as a "soft-shell" crab.

BUTTERED BAKED CRAB BETTERTON

Betterton was once a beach resort, drawing sun worshippers from Baltimore via the steamboats that connected the two locations. The steamboat has long been gone, but what remains is this delicious crab casserole. I know you're going to love it.

1   medium green pepper, chopped
1   medium onion, chopped
1   cup chopped celery
1   tablespoon vegetable oil
1   pound crabmeat
1   pound shrimp, cooked and cut up
½   teaspoon salt
½   teaspoon black pepper
1   teaspoon Worcestershire sauce
1   cup mayonnaise
1   cup buttered breadcrumbs

Sauté the green pepper, onion and celery in vegetable oil. Add crabmeat, shrimp, salt, black pepper, Worcestershire sauce, and mayonnaise, mix thoroughly and put into a casserole. Top with the breadcrumbs. Bake at 400°F until brown, about 15 to 20 minutes.

Serves 6 to 8.

For generations, the Chesapeake and its inhabitants have kept a relatively low profile, with many of their classic recipes and cooking preparations locked away. One thing that has not been locked away is crab art. The people of the Chesapeake are fun-loving, warm and welcoming, and they accept life on life's terms. This simplicity spills over into the signs of the crab.

13

CRISFIELD BILL'S GRILLED SOFT-SHELL CRABS

Soft-shell crabs may be deep fried in hot oil or simply sautéed in butter. Some aficionados believe that the simpler the better. Well, it doesn't get any simpler than this—you gotta taste it for yourself!

- **4** **tablespoons deli-style mustard**
- **3** **tablespoons melted butter**
- **8** **prime soft-shell crabs, dressed**

Once charcoals have stopped flaming, mix mustard with enough melted butter to get a liquid paste. Brush on the crabs. Place on grill for 2 minutes on each side. Serve immediately.

Serves 4.

Soft-shells are graded by the size of the shell span from point to point:

Medium: 2.5 to 4.0 inches
Hotel: 4.0 to 4.5 inches
Prime: 4.5 to 5.0 inches
Jumbo: 5.0 to 5.5 inches
Whales: over 5.5 inches

MD Blue Crab Salad on the Half Shell

🦀 *Dee T. Van Nest of Annapolis, Maryland took home the grand prize award at the 50th Annual National Hard Crab Derby, 1997, Crisfield, Maryland. Congratulations, Dee!*

CRAB SALAD:
- 1 **pound backfin crabmeat**
- 1 **avocado cut into small dice**
- **juice of 1 lemon**
- 3 **tablespoons plain nonfat yogurt**
- 3 **tablespoons light sour cream**
- 1½ **tablespoons finely chopped fresh parsley**
- 1 **tablespoon chopped fresh chives**
- 1 **teaspoon Old Bay seasoning**
- 2 **drops hot pepper sauce**
- 2 **tablespoons capers, drained**

Inspect crabmeat for shell. Set aside. Combine avocado with lemon juice. Mix yogurt, sour cream, parsley, chives, Old Bay seasoning, pepper sauce and capers. Add avocado and lemon juice to yogurt/sour cream mixture. Gently fold into the crab, trying not to break up lumps of crabmeat.

LACY SHELLS:
- 1¼ **cups coarsely grated Parmigiano-Reggiano cheese**
- 2 **sheets baking paper**

Preheat oven to 350°F. Place 2 tablespoons of cheese forming a circle about 3 inches in diameter on a parchment-covered baking sheet. Repeat to create 12 "lacy shells." Bake approximately 10 minutes or until brown. Remove immediately from sheet.

You'll have no trouble getting people to the table with this one. What I like about it is that you don't need anything else. Well, a glass of Chardonnay is a nice accompaniment!

SILKEN SAUCE, ACCOMPANIMENTS & SERVICE:
- ½ **cup whipping cream**
- 2 **tablespoons chili sauce**
- 1 **tablespoon Old Bay seasoning (or to taste)**
- ½ **pound baby lettuce**
- 12 **chive leaves**

Whip cream until slightly thick and add chili sauce and Old Bay. Continue beating until soft peaks are formed. Arrange lettuce on six salad plates, top with one lacy shell, and mound crab salad on shell. Position another shell on top with a few sprigs of chives. Garnish shell, salad and plate with a few dollops of sauce. Serve immediately.

Serves 6.

FULL TILT TUCKAHOE BRIDGE SOUP

🦀 *This is a very simple and quick soup. Whether you entertain the bridge club at noon or have a few friends in for luncheon, there's not enough Scotch in here to worry about.*

2　tablespoons finely chopped onion
3　tablespoons butter
½　teaspoon salt
　　freshly ground black pepper
1　pound backfin crabmeat
3　cups milk
½　cup heavy cream
2　tablespoons Scotch whisky
　　chopped fresh parsley

Cook the onion in the butter until transparent. Stir in the salt and pepper and cook over low heat for 10 minutes, stirring occasionally. Add the crabmeat and milk and cook in a double boiler over boiling water for 15 minutes. Add the heavy cream, and when the mixture is piping hot, stir in the Scotch whisky. Serve immediately garnished with chopped parsley.

Serves 8.

Summertime is crab time in Bay Country. There is little doubt that few social events don't include some "crab-talk" in one form or another. It seems that everyone is catching them, cooking them, eating them, or thinking about them.

NEW BAY CRAB CAKES W/GINGER LIME SAUCE

For a cooling patio lunch, serve New Bay Crab Cakes topped with a cool ginger lime sauce. Hot twist rolls, made from a mix, are a tasty accompaniment. For dessert, offer strawberry ice cream and refreshing ice tea garnished with fresh mint. Need more?

⅔ **cup mayonnaise**
1 **tablespoon lime juice**
¼ **teaspoon cayenne pepper**
1 **pound crabmeat**
1 **cup dry breadcrumbs, divided**
1 **jar (2 ounces) chopped pimiento, drained**
2 **tablespoons minced green onions**
1 **teaspoon chopped cilantro**
2 **tablespoons butter**
   Ginger Lime Sauce (recipe below)

Mix mayonnaise, lime juice and red pepper. Add crabmeat, ½ cup of breadcrumbs, pimientos and green onions. Form into 8 patties and coat in remaining breadcrumbs. Cook patties in butter in a large nonstick skillet over medium heat 3 minutes per side or until browned and heated through. Serve immediately with Ginger Lime Sauce (recipe below).

Serves 4.

GINGER LIME SAUCE:
½ **cup mayonnaise**
¼ **cup sour cream**
1 **tablespoon lime juice**
2 **teaspoons grated lime peel**
½ **teaspoon ground ginger**

Mix all ingredients. Serve with New Bay Crab Cakes. Makes ¾ cup.

To start a war in Chesapeake Bay Country, just stick your chin out and defiantly complete this sentence: "The only place to get really good crab cakes is . . ." I snapped this photo at Paul's, on the South River, Riva, Maryland. You know I wouldn't think of having Thanksgiving without crab cakes.

J.O. No. 1 Crab Cakes

🦀 *J.O. Spice Company of Baltimore, Maryland, has an excellent line of spices and herbs. Their No. 2 crab seasoning is used by many of the crab houses for steaming crabs. I suggest you try J.O. No. 1 for these wonderful crab cakes!*

1 **pound crabmeat (backfin or lump)**
1 **teaspoon J.O. No. 1 seasoning**
1 **tablespoon mayonnaise**
1 **tablespoon Worcestershire sauce**
1 **tablespoon chopped fresh parsley**
1 **tablespoon baking powder**
1 **egg beaten well**
2 **slices of bread with crusts removed, broken into small pieces and moistened slightly with milk**

Mix all ingredients and shape into cakes. Fry quickly until brown.

*C*hesapeake cooking began in 1608 when Captain John Smith guided his ship into the mouth of the Chesapeake Bay and landed in what was to become Jamestown, Virginia.

DAMES QUARTER CRAB CAKES

🦀 *Dames Quarter is a tiny hamlet in Somerset County on Maryland's lower Eastern Shore, and as with most communities that line the Chesapeake Bay, if you spend any time there you'll find good crab cakes. See if you don't agree.*

  1 **pound lump crabmeat**
  ½ **cup soft whole wheat breadcrumbs**
  ⅓ **cup chopped onion**
  ⅓ **cup chopped celery**
  2 **tablespoon mayonnaise**
  1 **tablespoon minced fresh basil**
  1 **teaspoon deli-style mustard**
  1 **teaspoon Worcestershire sauce**
  ⅛ **teaspoon cayenne pepper**
  1 **egg, beaten**
    vegetable cooking spray

Combine everything but the vegetable cooking spray in a bowl. Divide the mixture into 6 equal portions and shape each into a thick patty. Cover and chill 1 hour. Coat a large nonstick skillet with cooking spray; place over medium-low heat until hot. Add patties and cook 5 minutes on each side or until golden brown.

Serves 6.

"Gently" is the key word in describing how to form a crab cake. Do not compact crab cakes too much. They should be held together loosely. I place mine on a baking sheet and refrigerate for about an hour before frying.

19

BARBARA SIEGERT'S CRAB DIP

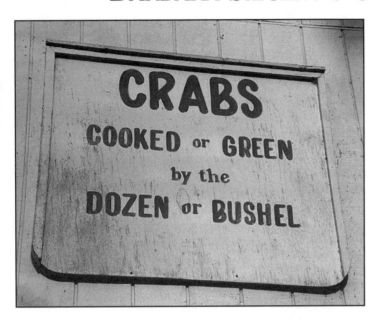

*S*igns like this one appear all around Bay Country. It simply means that you can purchase crabs both steamed and live. Although blue crabs are named for their brilliant blue claws, the body of the crab is olive drab with a white underside.

🦀 *This crab dip was a favorite in the Chesapeake Bay Maritime Museum's Best Ever Crab Recipe Contest. I know you'll find it easy to prepare and delicious. Source: Barbara Siegert, Grasonville, Maryland.*

- 28 **ounces cream cheese, softened**
- 1 **cup grated Parmigiano-Reggiano cheese, divided**
- ½ **teaspoon lemon juice**
- 4 **tablespoons mayonnaise**
- 1 **teaspoon garlic salt**
- 1 **pound crabmeat**

In a bowl, mix everything but the crabmeat, saving a little of the grated cheese for the top. Add the crabmeat and mix thoroughly. Place in a baking dish and top with the remaining grated cheese. Bake at 350°F for 30 minutes.

Serve with Tostitos.

Serves 12.

POOR MAN'S CRAB SEASONING

Every region of the Chesapeake has its own way of preparing its delicacies, but nothing compares to a peppery pile of steamed crabs fresh from the Bay liberally seasoned with this spicy concoction. This is one you can make at home. Feel free to adjust the amount of pepper you use. I like mine hot and spicy!

- 3 tablespoons paprika
- 2 tablespoons salt
- 1-2 tablespoons garlic powder
- 1 teaspoon black pepper
- 1 tablespoon onion powder
- 1 tablespoon cayenne pepper
- 1 tablespoon dried leaf oregano
- 1 tablespoon dried leaf thyme

Mix together and store air-tight. Shake well before using.

Makes about ⅔ cup.

Given the amount of crab and other seafood that is prepared in Chesapeake kitchens, the distinctive aroma of this seasoning scents the air on many a humid day. We call it Summer's Perfume.

TYLER CREEK GRILLED SOFT-SHELL CRABS

Crab signs have always been a source of inspiration for me. After logging more than one hundred thousand miles on Chesapeake Bay back roads, I only have to see a sign like this to have the urge strike, and you guessed it: it's crab for lunch.

🦀 *Soft-shells are referred to by a number of terms including peelers, red signs, sally crabs, busters, buckrams, and ranks. Regardless of what you call them, be sure and call me when these babies come off the grill.*

> 12 **soft-shell crabs**
> **Soft Crab Marinade (recipe follows)**

Liberally baste bottom sides of crabs with marinade and carefully place, bottom side down, on barbecue grill. Cook over a slow fire at least 12 inches from coals for 5 minutes. Liberally baste tops of crabs with marinade, turn carefully, and grill 5 minutes more.

Serves 6.

SOFT CRAB MARINADE:
> 1 **cup salad oil**
> 2 **tablespoons white vinegar**
> 2 **teaspoons salt**
> 6 **teaspoons fresh tarragon leaves**
> 1 **teaspoon lemon pepper seasoning**
> 1 **teaspoon lemon juice**
> 3 **cloves garlic, chopped**

Mix ingredients together. Let stand several hours at room temperature to let flavors blend before using.

Makes 1 cup marinade.

PUNGOTEAGUE CRAB CAKES

If carefully mixed, these crab cakes will be light and fluffy and of a delicate flavor. I find that the claw meat of the crab adds yet another dimension to this wonderful and tasty recipe.

- 4 **slices bread**
- ½ **cup olive oil**
- ½ **teaspoon salt**
-    **dash of paprika**
- 1 **teaspoon Worcestershire sauce**
- ⅛ **teaspoon dry mustard**
- 2 **eggs, separated**
- 2 **tablespoons chopped fresh parsley**
- 1 **pound backfin crabmeat**
- 1 **pound claw meat**

Trim crusts from bread slices, lay slices on a flat platter and pour olive oil over them. Let stand 1 hour, and then pull apart lightly with two forks. To the small bits of bread add salt, paprika, Worcestershire sauce, dry mustard, yolks of eggs and crabmeat and mix lightly with a fork. Beat egg whites until stiff and fold into crab mixture. Shape into 12 cakes. Brown in a hot frying pan just brushed with olive oil.

Serves 12.

The community of Pungoteague is on Virginia's lower Eastern Shore. It dates from 1660 and its name is derived from the Algonquian pongotecku, "river of the sandfly."

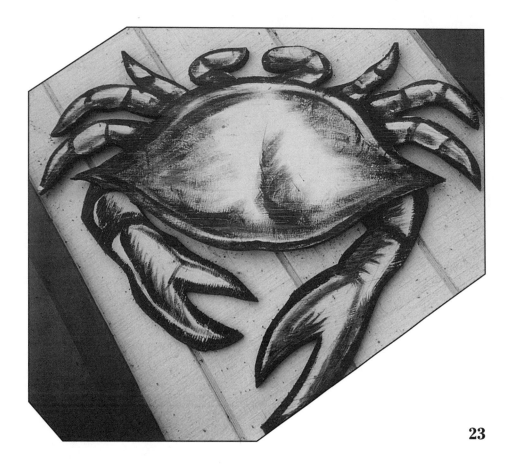

DEAL ISLAND DEVILED CRAB

Back in the 1960s and '70s, deviled crab dishes appeared on many menus around Bay Country. I found it easy to pop into a tavern for a cold beer and a delicious deviled crab. That tradition has disappeared since those early days, but when I spied this sign along the highway, guess what I had for lunch?

🦀 *Deal Island is a sandy and marshy lowland and was once considered "fit only for the Devil"; hence, it was called Devils Island by its earliest inhabitants. Today, it's home base to the last working skipjack fleet in America.*

  2 **cups corn flakes, crushed slightly**
1½ **cups grated American cheese**

Blend:
  1 **tablespoon lemon juice**
  2 **teaspoons dry mustard**
  2 **tablespoons Worcestershire sauce**
  2 **large eggs, beaten**

Add and mix carefully:
  3 **tablespoons chopped green onion**
  8 **ounces crabmeat**
  3 **cups mashed potatoes**

Mix the cornflakes and American cheese well and set aside. Blend the lemon juice, dry mustard, Worcestershire sauce and eggs. Add the green onion, crabmeat and mashed potatoes. Make this mixture into small round balls and roll in the cornflake/cheese mixture. Bake at 350°F until golden brown.

TAPPAHANNOCK BRIDGE CRAB SALAD

🦀 *Without a doubt, salads are my favorite dish, both to eat and prepare. I guess that's because I love my herb garden, and anytime I have an excuse to go out back and harvest fresh herbs, I do.*

- 1 **pound backfin crabmeat**
- ½ **cup sour cream**
- 1 **cup grated cheddar cheese**
- 1 **hard-boiled egg, chopped fine**
- 6 **slices bacon fried crisp, crumbled**
- 1 **teaspoon minced onion**
- 2 **tablespoons minced fresh dill weed**
- 1 **tablespoon minced fresh basil**
  salt and pepper to taste

Gently mix crabmeat, sour cream, cheese, egg, bacon, onion, dill weed, basil and salt and pepper to taste. Toss with salad mix.

Serves 6.

SALAD MIX:
- 12 **leaves buttercrunch lettuce**
- ½ **head iceberg lettuce, torn in pieces**
- 6 **small spinach leaves, torn in pieces**
- 6 **yellow Roma tomatoes, cut in half**

The name Tappahannock is a variation of Rappahannock, derived from the Algonquian word meaning "on the rise and fall of water" or "on the running water." Dorchester is a county on Maryland's Eastern Shore.

OLE VIRGINNEY CRAB CLAW SOUP

Blue crabs (Callinectus Sapidus) have brought fame to the Chesapeake Bay, and rightly so. I think they are the best tasting crabs available. If you want to try a great-tasting soup, give this version a try. It's sweet, flavorful and rewarding.

2	tablespoons butter
1	tablespoon all-purpose
2	eggs, hard-boiled and sieved
1	teaspoon grated lemon rind
2	cups light cream
2	cups milk
1½	pounds crabmeat from claws
1	teaspoon Worcestershire sauce
2	tablespoons sherry
	salt and freshly ground black pepper
4	tablespoons minced fresh parsley

Blend butter and flour in the top of a double boiler over simmering water. Stir in eggs and lemon rind. Stir in cream and milk alternately, a little at a time; continue stirring until smooth and slightly thickened. Add crabmeat and let simmer for 5 minutes. Stir in Worcestershire sauce and sherry, then season to taste with salt and pepper. Serve in heated soup bowls with a sprinkling of parsley.

Serves 10.

I snapped this photo in St. Michaels, Maryland, just outside the world-famous Crab Claw Restaurant. Now you can visit there and try the house version of crab soup or try this Ole Virginney style soup. Either way, you're in for a treat.

CRAB MEDALLIONS ROCKEFELLER-CAJUN STYLE

🦀 *This recipe by Ron Sasiela was a runner-up in the 1997 Best Ever Crab Recipe Contest held by Chesapeake Bay Maritime Museum in St. Michaels, Maryland. It's a winner.*

10	**ounces (1 package) fresh spinach or thawed frozen spinach**
¼	**cup chopped shallots**
¼	**cup chopped celery**
⅓	**cup chopped fresh parsley**
2	**tablespoons fennel seed**
1	**tablespoons anise seed**
1	**teaspoon Accent**
1	**teaspoon coarse kosher salt**
½	**teaspoon freshly ground black pepper**
¼	**teaspoon ground cayenne pepper or to taste**
3	**tablespoons olive oil**
⅓	**cup Pernod**
1	**pound crabmeat**
1	**large egg and 1 egg white, beaten**
3	**cups fresh whole wheat breadcrumbs, slightly dried (about 8-10 slices)**
	water to adjust consistency
	canola oil for deep fat or pan frying
	Garnishes: Tabasco-seasoned cocktail sauce or tartar sauce, parsley sprigs, lime wedges

Chop about 8 ounces of the spinach, reserving about 2 ounces of whole leaves for garnishing.

Sauté shallots, celery, parsley, fennel seed, anise seed, Accent, kosher salt, black pepper, and cayenne pepper in olive oil for 3 minutes over medium-high heat uncovered—enjoy the aroma coming from the pan! Remove from heat. Add the Pernod and chopped spinach and fold in the crabmeat with a two-tine fork so as not to reduce the size of the crab chunks. Add the egg mixture and stir; then add one third of the breadcrumbs and stir. If the mixture is too stiff to form into flattened balls, slowly drizzle in some water, always taking care to keep the lumps of crab as large as possible.

Shaping the medallions is important and should be done as follows:

Dampen hands with cold water. Divide out a heaping tablespoon of mixture. Place it between your hands and compress it firmly but gently; some moisture will be transferred from your hands to the mixture. Dredge this "medallion" in breadcrumbs to achieve an even, complete coating—this is important to keep the medallions extra crisp. Some of the spinach will show through the crumbs. Set medallions aside for about 15 minutes to allow the crumbs to absorb the surface moisture and help hold their delicate shape.

Fry at 330-350°F in oil until golden brown—about 2 to 3 minutes. Do not allow the oil to cool by trying to cook too many at once, as that will make them excessively oily.

Drain them on paper towels and keep warm (140°F) until ready to be served.

Serve with Tabasco-seasoned cocktail sauce or tartar sauce and garnish with sprigs of parsley and lime wedges, all placed on a bed of the remaining whole spinach leaves.

Serves 6.

I took this photograph while visiting Eastport near downtown historic Annapolis. I love the creativity different restaurants use to say "We have steamed crabs today!"

BEST BACKFIN CRAB CAKES

🦀 *This recipe was runner-up at the Coast Day 1997 Crab Cook-Off. The award went to Char Ann Smith of Bishopville, Maryland.*

- 2 **large eggs, beaten**
- 2 **tablespoons parsley flakes**
- 2 **teaspoons Old Bay seasoning**
- 2 **teaspoons French's mustard**
- 2 **teaspoons dry mustard**
- 2 **tablespoons Worcestershire sauce**
- 2 **teaspoons lemon juice**
- 1 **teaspoon salt**
- ¼ **teaspoon pepper**
- 2 **pounds jumbo lump crabmeat**
- 4 **tablespoons Miracle Whip salad dressing**
  cracker crumbs

Beat eggs. Add parsley flakes, Old Bay seasoning, mustards, Worcestershire sauce, lemon juice, salt and pepper. Combine with crabmeat and Miracle Whip. Shape into 12 balls and roll in cracker crumbs. Fry in oil or broil in 375°F oven for 20 minutes.

Serves 6.

*W*ant *a crab cake? You bet. I spotted this scene in Fredericksburg, Virginia, on the side of the building at Barefoot Green's Seafood Market.*

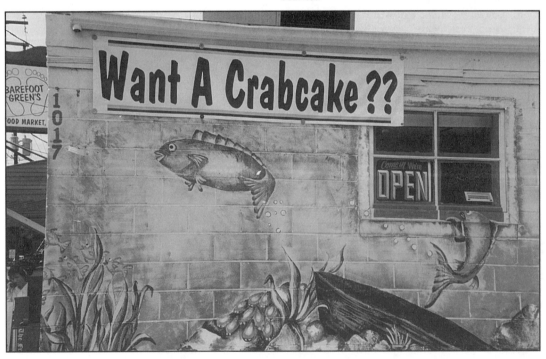

28

ST. CLEMENT'S ISLAND CRAB RAVIGOTE

A ravigote is a piquant sauce. It comes in a variety of forms, hot or cold. This recipe was created to give a lift to the crab, and you'll find it exciting.

1	pound crabmeat
2	tablespoons chopped sweet pickle
2	tablespoons lemon juice
¼	teaspoon salt
	dash of pepper
1	hard-boiled egg, chopped fine
1	tablespoon chopped fresh parsley
2	tablespoons chopped onion
¼	cup mayonnaise
2	tablespoons chopped stuffed olives
¼	teaspoon paprika
	pimiento strips

Combine crabmeat, pickle, lemon juice, salt, pepper, egg, parsley and onion. Place on salad greens. Combine mayonnaise, olives, and paprika; spread over the crab mixture. Chill. Garnish with pimiento strips.

Serves 6.

A quick drive from just about any town in the Chesapeake region will get you into crab country. Next time you're driving through the area, notice the ways crabs are displayed on buildings and trucks.

29

OLD POINT COMFORT SHE-CRAB SOUP

ABC—*Always Buy Crabs! See how easy it is to get confused? And why I am always walking sideways?*

🦀 *Every school child has heard of Hampton Roads, the scene of the battle between the Civil War ironclads Monitor and Merrimac. This battle was fought in sight of Fort Monroe, located on Old Point Comfort. Now there will be another battle if you forget to pass the sherry.*

2   tablespoons butter
1   tablespoon all-purpose
1   quart milk
1   pound crabmeat
5   drops onion juice
¼   teaspoon mace
¼   teaspoon pepper
1   lemon, grated rind only
½   teaspoon salt
4   tablespoons dry sherry
¼   pint heavy cream, whipped

In the top of double boiler, melt butter and blend with flour until smooth. While stirring constantly, slowly add the milk. Then add crabmeat, onion juice, mace, pepper, lemon rind, and salt, and cook over low heat for 20 minutes. Serve in warm cups with one tablespoon of sherry and a topping of whipped cream.

Serves 6.

ANNIE'S HOSTESS CRAB DELIGHT

This recipe was created by my friend Annie Hendricks of Alexandria, Virginia. it first appeared in The Official Crab Eater's Guide. *We like it so much we printed it again. Thanks, Annie.*

3	cups cooked rice
1	pound crabmeat
¼	cup minced onion
¼	cup chopped fresh parsley
¼	cup chopped pimiento
3	eggs, slightly beaten
2	cups milk
1	cup grated sharp cheese
1	teaspoon Worcestershire sauce
	Shrimp Sauce (recipe below)

Gently combine all ingredients. Place in a buttered 8 x 11-inch baking pan. Bake 35 to 45 minutes at 325°F. Cut into squares and serve with Shrimp Sauce.

SHRIMP SAUCE:

2	cans cream of shrimp soup
1	cup sour cream
1	teaspoon lemon juice
½	cup shrimp, cooked and cut up

Blend all ingredients and warm slowly over low heat, preferably in an iron skillet. Do not boil.

Serves 8 to 10.

A crab's sex can be determined by the shape of the abdomen or "apron" on the underside of the crab. A male crab has an apron shaped like an inverted "T," while an adult female's is more triangular.

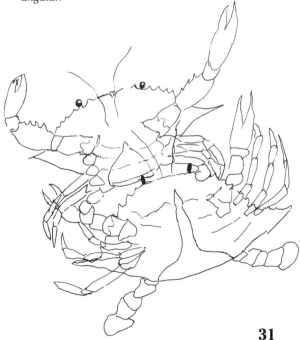

31

HOBO FARM GARLIC CRABS

The secret ingredient in this recipe is the crystallized ginger, sometimes called candied ginger because the ginger slices have been preserved in a sugar-salt mixture. Crystallized ginger can be found in Asian markets and many supermarkets.

24	blue crabs
	salt and pepper to taste
6	cloves garlic, slivered
6	tablespoons chopped crystallized ginger
4	tablespoons olive oil
1½	cups water
	melted butter for dipping

Remove top shells, front plates and bottom flaps of crabs. Remove anything that is not white meat. Leave the large claws attach to the bodies.

Place crabs in a large pot in four layers, sprinkling each layer with salt, pepper, garlic slivers, ginger and one tablespoon olive oil. Pour in water and cover.

Steam for 8 to 10 minutes or until claws turn red. Serve crabs and broth with melted butter for dipping.

Serves 4.

I snapped this photo on Deal Island on Maryland's lower Eastern Shore, whose history dates to 1675. Today a visitor can get a vision of what Deal Island was like—and how much it has changed—by traveling down the main road from Chance to Wenona. Many of the houses are in the single-gable style, while others are charming Victorians. Older trees and old-fashioned shrubs and flowers fill the yards. What attracts me are signs like this that tell yet another story.

CHAPTER 2
Crabby Crisfield

BYRDTOWN SOFT-SHELL CRABS

🦀 *The almond, the kernel of the fruit of the almond tree, is grown extensively in California. Toasting almonds before using them in recipes intensifies their flavor and adds crunch. Feel free to add extra toasted almonds as a garnish.*

1	cup sliced almonds
1	cup all-purpose flour
1	teaspoon salt
½	teaspoon pepper
½	teaspoon cayenne pepper
12	soft-shell crabs
1	cup milk
3	tablespoons butter
3	tablespoons vegetable oil

Preheat oven to 325°F. Spread almonds on a small baking sheet and toast in oven, stirring once or twice, until lightly browned, about 5 minutes. Immediately transfer to a plate to cool.

In a food processor, combine toasted almonds, flour, salt, pepper, and cayenne. Process until almonds are finely ground, about 30 seconds. Place this almond flour in a large bowl.

One at a time, dip half the crabs into the milk, then dredge lightly in the almond flour. In a large skillet, heat 1½ tablespoons each butter and oil over medium-high heat until hot but not smoking. Add coated crabs and cook, turning once, until golden brown, about 3 minutes per side. Drain on paper towels. Repeat with remaining crabs.

Serves 4.

The town of Crisfield, Maryland, is so crabby even the police department uniform displays a crab. If you are ever driving down Main Street, stay under the speed limit or a crab will get ya!

CRAB-AND-LEEK BISQUE JOHNSON CREEK

🦀 *A bisque is a thick, rich soup, usually containing lobster, crab or crayfish. I suggest you serve it piping hot with cornbread on the side and make a meal of it.*

- 3 leeks (about 1½ pounds)
- 1 stick butter
- 2 cloves garlic, minced
- ½ cup all-purpose flour
- 4 cups chicken broth
- ½ cup dry white wine
- 2 cups half-and-half
- 8 ounces crabmeat
- ½ teaspoon salt
- ½ teaspoon ground white pepper
     sliced leeks for garnish

Remove roots, tough outer leaves, and green tops from leeks. Split leeks in half, wash, and cut halves into thin slices. Melt butter in a Dutch oven over medium-high heat. Add leeks and garlic, and cook until tender. Add flour, stirring until smooth. Then cook 1 minute, stirring constantly. Gradually add broth and wine; cook over medium heat, stirring constantly, until mixture is thickened (about 4 minutes). Stir in half-and-half, crabmeat, salt and pepper. Garnish with sliced leeks.

Serves 6.

*W*orkers cull crabs—separate the smaller ones from the larger. In Crisfield, as it is all over Bay Country, "the bigger the crab the bigger the price."

DERBY DAY CRAB RICE

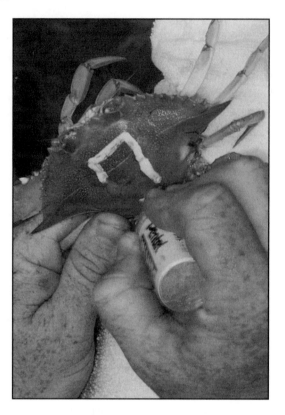

🦀 *When I "plate" Derby Day Crab Rice, I pile it high and then top it with a crispy pan-fried soft-shell crab. It's sophistication and simplicity all in one.*

3	tablespoons butter
2	cups uncooked rice
1	bunch green onions, chopped
2	tomatoes, peeled and chopped
3	cloves garlic, mashed
2	tablespoons minced fresh parsley
2	peeled green chiles, chopped
¼	cup finely chopped celery
1	pound crabmeat
4½	cups water
	salt and pepper

Fry rice lightly in butter in a large kettle. Add all other ingredients and simmer 30 minutes, or until all liquid has been absorbed.

Serves 6.

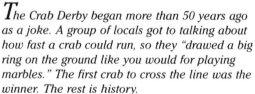

The Crab Derby began more than 50 years ago as a joke. A group of locals got to talking about how fast a crab could run, so they "drawed a big ring on the ground like you would for playing marbles." The first crab to cross the line was the winner. The rest is history.

LILY'S CRAB CAKES

🦀 *Lillian Flugrath of Columbia, Maryland, won first prize in the crab cake division and grand prize overall at the 48th National Hard Crab Derby, Crisfield, Maryland.*

1   **pound backfin crabmeat**
2   **tablespoons dried parsley flakes**
1   **slice white bread made into crumbs**
¼   **teaspoon dried lemon peel**
1   **egg**
1   **egg yolk**
3   **tablespoons mayonnaise**
2   **teaspoons horseradish**
2   **teaspoons horseradish mustard**
1   **tablespoon Worcestershire sauce**
1   **tablespoon white wine Worcestershire
      sauce**
5   **drops Tabasco sauce**
⅛   **teaspoon freshly ground black pepper
      vegetable oil for frying**

Put crabmeat in a large bowl (if it is very wet, gently pat dry with a paper towel). Add parsley, breadcrumbs and lemon peel and toss lightly with a fork. In a separate bowl or glass measuring cup, beat egg and egg yolk lightly with a wire whisk. Add mayonnaise and beat until smooth. Add horseradish, horseradish mustard, Worcestershire sauce, white wine Worcestershire sauce, Tabasco sauce and pepper and beat until smooth again. Pour half of the liquid mixture over the crabmeat mixture and toss lightly with a fork. Add the remaining liquid ingredients and toss lightly again. Gently pat crab cake mixture into patties, about ⅓ cup each. Chill crab cakes a half hour before frying. Heat a heavy iron skillet and add ¼ inch vegetable oil. When oil is hot, fry crab cakes over medium heat until golden brown on both sides, 4-6 minutes per side. Drain on paper towels.

Serve with crackers or rolls and your favorite sauce.

Serves 6.

*B*eing a judge in a cooking contest can be a lot of work. For example, I had to sit at a long table for more than 5 hours sampling everything from crab pizza, crab soup, crab salad, crab appetizers, and crab tarts to Lily's Crab Cakes. I can't wait to go back to work!

JENKINS CREEK CRAB CAKES À LA MATT

"There is no doubt about it—the addition of mayonnaise produces a better crab cake." — *source unknown.*

1	**pound lump crabmeat**
¼	**cup finely chopped fresh parsley**
2	**slices white bread, crust removed, made into crumbs**
¼	**teaspoon baking powder**
½	**teaspoon Old Bay seasoning**
	pinch of salt
	pinch of white pepper
1	**teaspoon dry mustard**
2	**tablespoons dry white wine**
	juice of 1 lemon
1	**tablespoon Worcestershire sauce**
¾	**cup mayonnaise**
2	**eggs, beaten lightly**
	oil for frying

In a medium mixing bowl, place crab, parsley, and breadcrumbs. Mix lightly with fingers. Dust the top of the mixture with baking powder and refrigerate. Mix Old Bay seasoning, salt, pepper, dry mustard, wine, lemon juice, and Worcestershire sauce. Blend with mayonnaise and eggs. Combine the mixtures. Gently pat into 8 cakes. Pan-fry until golden brown.

Serves 4.

Jenkins Creek is little more than a narrow channel leading to the Crisfield County wharf and launching ramp. While some small, shallow-draft boats might find a few places to anchor, this popular creek is used as water access for fishermen.

CRAB PICKER'S CRAB SOUP

Crab soups are one of my favorite foods. While working on my last book, The Chesapeake Bay Waterside Dining Guide, *I found my way to 212 restaurants and had crab soup in most of them. This recipe is rich and creamy and is traditionally reserved for more formal dinners, but I can eat it any time of day!*

1	onion diced
¼	cup diced celery
6	tablespoons butter
5	tablespoons all-purpose flour
1	quart milk
1	pint light cream
3	cups canned tomatoes
	pinch of baking soda
	salt and pepper to taste
1	pound crabmeat
	seafood seasoning
¼	cup sherry

Combine onion and celery in a 2-quart saucepan with butter; cook until soft. Remove from heat and stir in flour smoothly. Return pan to heat and add milk a little at a time, stirring and cooking until the mixture thickens. Add cream a little at a time, stirring constantly. Bring to a boil and boil for 3 minutes, continuing to stir. Strain tomatoes through a sieve into a bowl, add baking soda, mix, stir into the cream sauce, and season with salt and pepper to taste. Add crabmeat and seafood seasoning. Reheat slowly, stirring and adding sherry.

Serves 4 to 6.

Smith Island, 12 miles west of Crisfield, Maryland, is a place of rugged beauty and old world charm. Captain John Smith, when he visited the island in 1608, gave it his name. The island is populated almost entirely by watermen, and in the summer, when it's crab picking time, the busiest place around is the ladies crabmeat co-op.

Photograph by Vince Lupo

TRAUGOTT'S SAUTÉED SOFT-SHELL CRABS

Herbal sauces can be hot or cold, used in cooking or added at serving time, and are often the element that sets one dish apart from another. If you use herbs to add flavor to the foods you serve, your reputation as a good cook is assured!

8   **prime soft-shell crabs, cleaned**
　　all-purpose flour for dredging
　　vegetable oil for frying
8   **pieces white toast**

HERB SAUCE:
1   **stick butter**
1   **teaspoon minced fresh parsley**
1   **teaspoon minced fresh tarragon**
1   **teaspoon minced fresh basil**
1   **teaspoon minced fresh chives**
½   **cup white wine**
　　juice of 1 lemon
　　salt and freshly ground white pepper

Lightly dredge crabs in flour. Heat oil in frying pan and sauté crabs 2 to 3 minutes on each side. Remove to a warm platter. Discard the oil. To make sauce, melt butter with parsley, tarragon, basil and chives in frying pan. Add wine, lemon juice, salt and freshly ground white pepper to taste. Cook until reduced by half. To serve, place crabs on toast and top with herb sauce.

Serves 4.

An isolated crab shanty sits across the shallow waters on Jenkins Creek. I spend many an evening here sitting out on the rickety pier watching the boats come in and the sun go down.

SOFT-SHELL CRABS BUSTER NELSON

The shallot, a small variety of onion that grows in clusters, is probably the most prized member of the onion family among cooks. I love shallots with soft-shell crabs. Their mild onion flavor doesn't overpower the crabs and lets their delicate taste shine through.

1½ **cups all-purpose flour**
1 **teaspoon salt**
½ **teaspoon freshly ground black pepper**
¼ **teaspoon cayenne pepper**
6 **hotel soft-shell crabs**
   cold milk
   peanut oil for frying

BUTTER SAUCE:
1 **stick butter**
2 **shallots, finely chopped**
1 **cup slivered, blanched almonds**
2 **teaspoons fresh lemon juice**
1 **teaspoon freshly ground white pepper**

Mix flour, salt, pepper and cayenne. Dip crabs in cold milk and then in the flour mixture. Heat ⅛ inch of oil in a frying pan and sauté 3 to 5 minutes on each side. Remove from pan and cover to keep warm.

Butter sauce: To make sauce, melt butter over medium heat in a 2-quart saucepan. Add shallots and slivered almonds. Cook just until the butter begins to brown, then remove the pan from the heat. With a slotted spoon, remove the shallots and almonds from the butter and set aside until serving time. Add the lemon juice and pepper and stir with a wooden spoon. The sauce will foam up. When the foaming subsides, return the pan to the heat and cook for 1 to 2 minutes or until the sauce turns a rich, golden brown. Remove from the heat.

To serve, place sautéed crabs on heated plates. Sprinkle with reserved shallots and almonds. Spoon about 1½ tablespoons of sauce over each crab.

Serves 2.

Strong early-morning winds delayed our departure from Kie Tyler's Crab Shanty on Jenkins Creek, but it didn't take long for Buster Nelson to pull in the crab scrape. The scrape is a lightweight type of "summertime" dredge with a toothless bottom bar and a long bag made of twine. Buster rakes through the grass to strain out peelers and soft-shell crabs.

THE MILLER'S WIFE SOFT-SHELL CRABS

🦀 *In French classical cuisine, food cooked à la meunière (literally "in the style of the miller's wife") is lightly coated in flour, fried in butter and sprinkled with lemon juice.*

8 **prime soft-shell crabs**
salt and pepper
lemon juice
2 **tablespoons deli-style mustard**
all-purpose flour for dredging
2 **tablespoons butter**
8 **teaspoons minced fresh parsley**
tartar sauce

Season crabs with salt, pepper and lemon juice. Brush underbellies with deli-style mustard. Dip both sides in flour. In a large frying pan, heat 2 teaspoons butter. Sauté crabs on both sides, about 2 minutes on each side. Sprinkle each with 1 teaspoon parsley. In a separate pan, heat 8 teaspoons butter and cook until a rich nutty brown. Pour 1 teaspoon butter over each crab. Serve with tartar sauce on the side.

Serves 4.

You know, it doesn't matter whether you're having soft-shell crabs, steamed crabs, deviled crabs, crab soup or crab cakes. Nothing goes with 'em like ice cold beer. Don't you agree?

CHESAPEAKE TRIANGLES

🦀 *This recipe by Lisa Perry was a favorite at the Best Ever Crab Recipe Contest. The crab dishes are evaluated on appearance, texture, originality and the appropriate use of crabs. When I prepared the dish at my crab lab, my guests were thrilled. Thanks, Lisa.*

5⅓ tablespoons unsalted butter
 ⅓ cup chopped shallots
 ⅔ cup dry vermouth
 1 package (3 ounces) cream cheese, softened
 3 teaspoons chopped fresh flat-leaf parsley
 1 teaspoon Old Bay seasoning
 2 teaspoons heavy cream
 3 lightly beaten egg yolks
 1 pound lump crabmeat
 ½ pound phyllo, thawed
     melted unsalted butter (approx. 1 stick)
     parsley sprigs and lemon slices
       to garnish

Melt ⅓ cup butter in sauté pan, add shallots, and cook till soft and golden. Add vermouth and boil till reduced to approximately ½ cup. Add cream cheese, parsley, Old Bay seasoning and cream. Remove from heat. Add egg yolks, stir until smooth and fold in crabmeat. Let cool.

Unwrap phyllo and keep covered with a slightly damp cloth. Place a sheet of phyllo on the work surface, brush well with melted butter, cover with a second sheet and brush with butter again. Cut into 5 strips approximately 3 inches wide. Place a heaping teaspoon of crab mixture on the bottom center of the first strip about an inch or so from the end. Fold a corner across the filling and fold as if folding a flag. Do not fold too tightly, as the filling expands a little.

Place triangles on a buttered cookie sheet and brush the tops with butter, continuing until all the filling is used. Triangles can be refrigerated for a day before baking.

Bake at 350°F for 20 to 25 minutes until golden brown and hot. Garnish with lemon slices and parsley sprigs. Serve hot or warm.

Serves 6.

When we test a recipe, more often than not we make a few changes in it. We add an ingredient here, take one out there, change a measure or two, lengthen or shorten cooking times, and so forth, all the while remaining faithful to the intent of the recipe's creator.

Photograph by Vince Lupo

TOP HAT CRAB AND CAVIAR

🦀 *When you use caviar in a dish like this, add it just before serving, otherwise the oil will discolor the crabmeat. My hat's off to the chef!*

1	**cup sour cream**
2	**tablespoons buttermilk**
½	**cup mayonnaise**
1	**pound crabmeat**
1½	**cups diced cucumber**
6	**tablespoons chopped fresh chives**
	juice of 1 lemon
	salt to taste
6	**fancy wine glasses**

GARNISH:

1	**container (4 ounces) salmon caviar**
6	**lemon slices**

In a bowl, thoroughly mix sour cream, buttermilk and mayonnaise. Toss crabmeat with this mixture to coat thoroughly; keep chilled. In another bowl, mix cucumber and chives. Sprinkle with lemon juice and salt and toss to blend. With a spoon, spread a layer of cucumber mixture in the bottom of each of the wine glasses. Next make a wider layer of crabmeat, then another layer of cucumber and another layer of crabmeat. Top with a splash of the sour cream dressing and decorate with salmon caviar and lemon slices.

Serves 6.

Hazel Cropper prepares to dig for backfin at the 51st Annual Hard Crab Derby in Crisfield, Maryland.

Photograph by Vince Lupo

44

CRAB AND BUNCHING ONION QUICHE

🦀 *If the only onions you've grown are from sets, you're missing out, because mild, sweet onions can't be grown that way. I suggest you try summer bunching onions. They're a perennial whose several tubular stems grow in a bunch throughout the season. Their delicate flavor is perfect for this quiche.*

1	baked pastry shell
1½	cups grated Gruyère cheese
2	tablespoons butter
7	bunching onions, chopped
8	ounces crabmeat
4	eggs
1	cup light cream
2	tablespoons lemon juice
1	teaspoon grated lemon peel
¼	teaspoon salt
¼	teaspoon dry mustard

Sprinkle the bottom of the pastry shell with half the cheese. In a frying pan, melt the butter. Add onions and cook until soft. Gently mix with the crabmeat and spoon evenly over the cheese in the pie shell. In a bowl, beat the eggs with the cream, lemon juice, lemon peel, salt, and mustard. Pour over the crab mixture. Sprinkle with the remaining cheese. Bake for 55 to 60 minutes at 325°F or until the center is set and firm. Let cool 15 minutes. Serve warm.

Serves 6.

One thing you will like about Crisfield is its dedication to the blue crab. You know about the police cars, the newspaper logo, the high school mascots, but did you know about all the street signs?

DAD'S CRAB CHOWDER

*T*his photo was taken at Peppy's Pub. The artwork is painted on a door leading out to the crab-eating deck that overlooks all of downtown Crisfield.

🦀 *This crab chowder is the house special at Price's Seafood in Havre de Grace, Maryland, where it's served in a disposable plastic bowl. It's chock full of minced vegetables, ground thyme, and crab lumps. Our Crab Lab taste testers all said, "This is one wonderful soup."*

1	stick butter
1	cup finely chopped onions
1	cup finely chopped celery
1	cup finely chopped carrots
1	pound crabmeat
½	teaspoon dry thyme
½	teaspoon freshly ground black pepper
1	cup clam juice
1	quart half-and-half
1	quart chicken broth
2	bay leaves
1	quart water
	salt to taste

Melt butter in soup kettle. Sauté onions, celery, and carrots until soft and golden. Add crabmeat, thyme, pepper, clam juice, half-and-half, chicken broth, bay leaves, water, and salt and cookover low heat for 35 minutes. Do not boil.

Serves 12.

APE HOLE CREEK CRAB IMPERIAL

🦀 *Yes, crabs. More specifically, the Atlantic blue crab, good old* Callinectes Sapidus, *the most celebrated (and consumed) product of the entire Chesapeake region. And you may call it Crab Imperial or Imperial Crab . . . but call me when it's ready.*

- 3 **tablespoons butter**
- 1 **tablespoon all-purpose flour**
- ½ **cup milk**
- 1 **teaspoon instant minced onion**
- 1½ **teaspoons Worcestershire sauce**
- 2 **slices white bread, crusts removed, cubed**
- ½ **cup mayonnaise**
- 1 **tablespoon lemon juice**
- ½ **teaspoon salt**
   a few turns of freshly ground pepper
- 1 **pound backfin crabmeat**
   paprika

In a medium saucepan, melt 1 tablespoon of the butter; mix in flour. Slowly add milk, stirring constantly to keep the mixture free of lumps. Cook, stirring, over medium heat until the mixture comes to a boil and thickens. Mix in onion, Worcestershire sauce, and bread cubes. Let cool. Fold in mayonnaise, lemon juice, salt, and pepper. In a skillet, heat the remaining 2 tablespoons of butter until lightly browned. Add the crabmeat and toss lightly. Combine crabmeat with the sauce mixture. Spoon into a buttered 2-quart casserole and sprinkle with paprika. Bake at 450°F for 10 to 15 minutes, or until hot, bubbly and golden brown on top.

Serves 6.

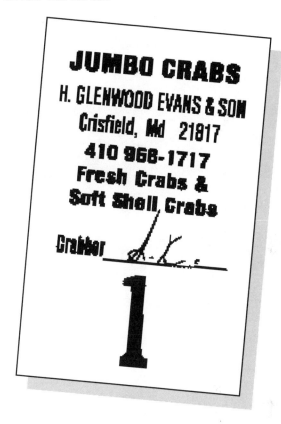

*O*nce crabs arrive at H. Glenwood Evans & Son, Crisfield, Maryland, the next step is to cull them. Workers pick over the catch and sort the crabs into baskets by size. The biggest and best are tagged number 1. Medium and lighter crabs are tagged number 2, and females are number 3.

SPAGHETTI WITH CRAB SAUCE

These folding chairs on the dock at H. Glenwood Evans won't sit idle for long. "Soon as them boys get the workboat unloaded, why we can sit down, relax and talk about all the crabs we caught today. We laid into a whole herd of 'em today."

🦀 *You don't have to be Italian to enjoy this delicious spaghetti. You'll like it regardless of your nationality. It's mighty good!*

½   **cup chopped onion**
½   **cup chopped celery**
3   **cloves garlic, finely chopped**
2   **tablespoons chopped fresh parsley**
4   **tablespoons melted butter**
1   **cup canned tomatoes**
1   **can (8 ounces) tomato sauce**
¼   **teaspoon salt**
½   **teaspoon paprika**
    dash of pepper
1   **pound crabmeat**
3   **cups cooked spaghetti**
    grated Parmigiano-Reggiano cheese

Cook onion, celery, garlic, and parsley in butter until tender. Add tomatoes, tomato sauce, salt, paprika and pepper. Simmer for 20 minutes, stirring occasionally. Add crabmeat; heat. Serve over spaghetti. Garnish with Parmigiano-Reggiano cheese.

Serves 6.

CRAB-STUFFED ROCKFISH WITH CAPER SAUCE

🦀 *Chesapeake. The name is Indian in origin, meaning "great shellfish bay," and great it is when you combine fresh crabmeat with a just-caught rockfish. The refinement of the Chesapeake comes across in this truly impressive dish.*

1	3-pound Maryland rockfish, cleaned and ready for stuffing
4	tablespoons butter
¼	cup chopped shallots
3	tablespoons chopped celery
8	ounces crabmeat
2	tablespoons chopped fresh parsley
	salt and pepper
1	cup breadcrumbs from fresh white bread
¼	cup light cream
	Caper Sauce (recipe follows)

Rinse rockfish thoroughly and dry. Melt butter and cook shallots and celery until tender. Add crabmeat, parsley, salt and pepper to taste, breadcrumbs and cream. Mix well. Fill cavity of fish loosely and sew with string. Bake in 400°F oven for about 35 minutes or until fish flakes. Remove the string before serving. Serve topped with Caper Sauce.

CAPER SAUCE:

3	tablespoons butter
⅓	cup all-purpose flour
1¼	cups milk
2	tablespoons capers, chopped
2	teaspoons vinegar from the caper jar
	salt and pepper

Put the butter in a microwave-safe bowl and cook on Full for 45 seconds. Stir in the flour. Pour in the milk and cook on Full for 3 minutes, beating after each minute. Stir in the capers and vinegar and season to taste with salt and pepper.

Crisfield is on the southernmost tip of Maryland's Eastern Shore, about halfway between Baltimore and Norfolk. The naturally picturesque setting is surrounded by marshlands and waterfront wildlife. If you haven't visited yet, you should—just look for flags like this!

BEST EVER CRAB CAKE

🦀 *This recipe is by Al Olinde, Salisbury, Maryland, who has his roots in Louisiana and a part of his heart here in "Bay Country." It's yet another illustration of the multi-styled crab cake. What you get with Al's crab cakes is a mouthful of pure crustacean delight.*

2-4 **tablespoons cracker crumbs**
½ **cup finely chopped green onions**
   Cajun seasoning or paprika
1 **pound lump crabmeat**
½ **cup sour cream**
1 **teaspoon Worcestershire sauce**
   dash of Tabasco sauce
   Lemon Butter Parsley Sauce
     (recipe follows)

Mix the cracker crumbs, green onions and a dash of Cajun seasoning or paprika. Using a rubber spatula, gently fold in the crabmeat, sour cream, Worcestershire sauce and Tabasco sauce. Form the mixture into six crab cakes and place on a baking sheet that has been sprayed with vegetable cooking spray or very lightly oiled. Sprinkle crab cakes with additional Cajun seasoning or paprika and bake for 10 to 15 minutes at 400°F. Top each serving with Lemon Butter Parsley Sauce.

LEMON BUTTER PARSLEY SAUCE:
1 **stick butter**
2 **tablespoons chopped fresh parsley**
1 **tablespoon lemon juice**
1 **tablespoon white wine**
½ **teaspoon salt**
½ **teaspoon pepper**
   dash of Tabasco sauce
   dash of Worcestershire sauce

Melt butter in saucepan and mix in parsley, lemon juice, white wine, salt, pepper, Tabasco sauce and Worcestershire sauce. Simmer briefly over low heat.
Serves 6.

Al Olinde was the grand prize winner of the 1990 Crab Cooking Contest. In that contest, this recipe was titled "Cajun Stuffed Crab with a Lemon Butter Parsley Sauce." Call it what you want—it's one of the best you'll ever try. The photo of the Crab World sign was snapped off Route 50 in Salisbury, Maryland.

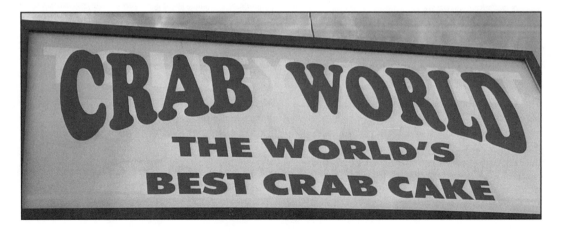

CRAB IN PISTOU SAUCE

🦀 *Pistou is a mixture of basil, crushed garlic and olive oil. It's the French version of Italy's pesto. For this recipe I've eliminated the garlic and added water chestnuts for crunch.*

12	large basil leaves, minced
2	tablespoons minced fresh parsley
1	egg
½	tablespoon salt
1	tablespoon wine vinegar
½	teaspoon deli-style mustard
½	cup olive oil
¼	cup vegetable oil
	lemon juice
8	ounces crabmeat
4	water chestnuts, sliced thin
	tomato and cucumber slices

Spin basil and parsley in a blender for about 1 minute; add egg, salt, vinegar and mustard, then slowly pour in both oils mixed together while continuing to blend. If mixture becomes thick before using all of the oil, add a few drops of the lemon juice. When sauce is thoroughly blended and the oil is completely used, taste for seasoning and add a few drops more lemon juice if needed. Mix this sauce into the crabmeat and stir in the sliced water chestnuts. Serve with tomato and cucumber slices as an appetizer.

Serves 4.

Most professional crab pickers can pick more than three pounds in 15 minutes. The all-time record is 4 pounds, 9 ounces by Betty Lou Middleton. Did you know that in 1992 a contest was held to crown the king of crab eaters? The title went to Frank Mackenzie of Annapolis, Maryland, who put away 55 crabs in 50 minutes.

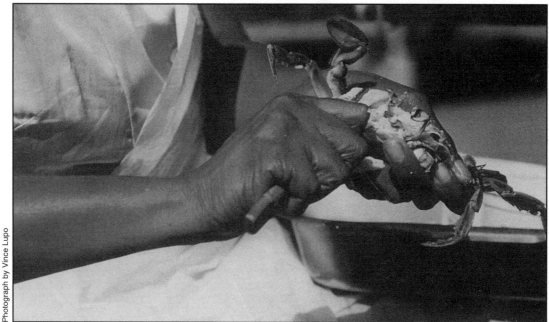

Photograph by Vince Lupo

SOFT-SHELL CRABS WITH LEMON BUTTER SAUCE

🦀 *You sometimes forget how easy soft-shell crabs are to prepare. What you won't forget is the raves you will receive from your dinner guest. This dish will make a hero out of you, I promise.*

6	**small fresh soft-shell crabs**
1	**stick margarine, melted**
	Lemon Butter Sauce (recipe follows)
	lemon halves for garnish
	fresh parsley for garnish
	paprika

Sauté crabs in margarine for 5 to 6 minutes or until lightly browned, turning once. Remove from heat and drain off margarine. Pour lemon butter sauce over crabs; return to heat and bring to boil. Reduce heat and simmer for 5 minutes. Garnish with lemon halves, parsley and paprika.

Serves 2.

LEMON BUTTER SAUCE:

4	**tablespoons melted butter**
¼	**cup lemon juice**
¼	**cup Worcestershire sauce**

Combine all ingredients and mix well. Makes ¾ cup.

*C*rab scrapes frame Hon's Crab Shanty on Jenkins Creek, Crisfield, Maryland.

MAKEPEACE SOFT CRAB MELT

🦀 *The intense aroma and flavor of basil (described variously as spicy, warm, pungent, sweet and clove-like) are a powerful reminder of a healthy, relaxed Bay Country lifestyle that revolves around the pleasures of the table. Basil's closest culinary ally is the tomato—now see what it does for soft-shell crabs.*

- 1 cup chopped fresh basil
- 1 small onion, finely diced
- ½ cup olive oil
- ¼ cup white vinegar
- 12 ½-inch slices of tomato
- 6 soft-shell crabs
- ½ cup all-purpose flour
  salt and freshly ground black pepper to taste
- 4 tablespoons clarified butter
- 6 slices rye bread
- 12 thin slices Gruyère cheese

Mix basil, onion, olive oil, and vinegar. Spread tomato slices on a large platter and ladle with basil dressing. Marinate for 2 hours, refrigerated. Dredge crabs in a mixture of flour, salt and pepper. In a large pan, sauté crabs in the clarified butter over medium heat for about 3 minutes on each side or until firm. Toast bread and top each slice with 2 tomato slices, a crab, and 2 cheese slices. Place under the broiler until the cheese is melted.

Serves 6.

*C*risfield, Maryland, is home to the John T. Handy Co., the largest shipper of soft-shell crabs in the world. Soft crabs can be shipped thousands of miles live and when frozen, they keep for months with little or no flavor loss.

Al Olinde's Crabmeat Louisiana

🦀 *This recipe by Al Olinde features the pairing of delicate fettuccine and lump crabmeat. Al's special recipe can be used as an appetizer, light lunch or smashing entrée.*

1	stick lightly salted butter
3	cups sliced mushrooms
1	cup chopped green onions
2	cloves garlic, minced
1	pound lump crabmeat
½	cup white wine
1½	cups heavy cream
	pinch of crushed red pepper
	pinch of salt
	cooked fettuccine or toast points

In a large skillet over high heat, sauté mushrooms, green onions and garlic in butter. Add crabmeat and wine and cook 2 to 3 minutes. Add cream and reduce sauce for 2 to 3 minutes. Season as desired with red pepper and salt.

Serve over cooked fettuccine as a main course or over toast points as an appetizer.

Serves 8 generously as an appetizer, or 4 as an entrée.

A worker at Smith Island ladies Crabmeat Co-op picks crabs. Here are some guidelines to help you pick: Pull off the claws by hand; pull off the back; take out the belly and eggs; cut off the legs; skim your crab knife across the top and pull the meat out with the knife.

Photograph by Vince Lupo

CHAPTER 3
Crab Pot Pourri

PORT OF SOLOMONS CRAB SOUFFLÉ

🦀 *I love preparing soufflés. They are easy to do and the results are spectacular. Try this recipe tonight and see what I mean.*

3	tablespoons butter
¼	cup all-purpose flour
1½	teaspoons dry mustard
1	cup milk
3	egg yolks, beaten
2	tablespoons chopped fresh parsley
2	tablespoons minced onion
1	tablespoon lemon juice
1	pound crabmeat
3	egg whites, beaten until stiff

Melt butter and blend in flour and dry mustard. Add milk gradually and cook until thick and smooth, stirring constantly.

Stir a little of this white sauce into the beaten egg yolks and then add the egg yolk mixture back into the white sauce, stirring constantly. Add parsley, onion, lemon juice, and crabmeat. Fold in egg whites. Place in a buttered 1½ quart casserole. Place casserole in a pan of hot water. Bake at 350°F for 1 hour or until soufflé is firm in the center. Serve without delay.

Serves 6.

This wooden cutout crab is a great tool for displaying cookbooks at the Chesapeake Bay Maritime Museum in St. Michaels, Maryland. If The Crab Cookbook *is not in your kitchen library, it should be!*

KINGSMILL CRAB SALAD IN ASPIC RINGS

🦀 *Herbs have been described as the soul of cooking and the praise of cooks. Used judiciously, they can transform a routine meal into a sensuous experience of tangy, spicy, refreshing flavors and crunchy textures.*

ASPIC:

2	**tablespoons unflavored gelatin**
½	**cup cold water**
1½	**cups tomato juice**
1	**teaspoon sugar**
½	**teaspoon salt**
½	**teaspoon Worcestershire sauce**
½	**teaspoon onion salt**
2	**tablespoons lemon juice**

CRAB SALAD:

8	**ounces crabmeat**
2	**tablespoons chopped onion**
1	**cup chopped celery**

1	**tablespoon lemon juice**
¼	**teaspoon salt**
	dash of pepper
¼	**cup mayonnaise**
	salad greens
	fresh herbs, your choice

Aspic: Soften gelatin in cold water for 5 minutes. Heat tomato juice to boiling; add gelatin and stir until dissolved. Add sugar, salt, Worcestershire sauce, onion salt and lemon juice. Place in 6 individual 3-ounce ring molds; chill until firm.

Crab Salad: Combine crabmeat, onion, celery, lemon juice, salt, pepper, and mayonnaise. Chill.

Assembling salad: Unmold aspic rings on salad greens. Fill centers with crab salad. Garnish with fresh herbs.

Serves 6.

"Crab pots are expensive, and it's nothing to set out $6,000 worth of them in the spring. I'll be lucky if I still got half of them by fall." — Wingate, Maryland, 1996

NANTICOKE RIVER CRAB CAKES

Photograph by Vince Lupo

*H*ere the author prepares another crab cake recipe in his "crab lab," Crisfield, Maryland, 1997.

🦀 *On crab cake heaven: You can talk to two dozen people and get two dozen answers, but one thing most agree on is, "I want a crab cake without any filler."*

1	**pound backfin crabmeat**
½	**cup mayonnaise**
2	**tablespoons deli-style mustard**
1	**egg, beaten**
1	**teaspoon butter**
1	**teaspoon olive oil**

Lightly mix all ingredients. Form into 6 cakes. Place in a small pan and gently sauté in the butter and olive oil. (Or try placing crab cakes in an oven-proof skillet without oil or butter. Place the skillet on a baking sheet and bake at 400°F for 15 to 20 minutes or until the cakes just start to brown.)

Serves 6.

STILLPOND CREEK CRAB PUFFS

🦀 *Stillpond is located about midway between Howell Point, at the mouth of the Sassafras River, and Norton Point. You'll find me located right at the oven door—I like my crab puffs while they're hot.*

- 2 **tablespoons butter**
- 2 **tablespoons all-purpose flour**
- ½ **teaspoon salt**
   dash of pepper
- 1 **cup milk**
- 2 **egg yolks, beaten**
- ¼ **teaspoon paprika**
- 1 **pound crabmeat**
- 1 **cup whipping cream, whipped**
- 2 **egg whites, beaten until stiff**

Melt butter; blend in flour, salt and pepper. Add milk gradually and cook until thick and smooth, stirring constantly. Stir a little of this white sauce into the egg yolks and then add egg yolk mixture to remaining white sauce, stirring constantly. Add paprika and crabmeat. Fold in whipped cream and beaten egg whites. Place in 6 buttered individual casseroles. Place the casseroles in a pan of hot water and bake at 350°F for 40 to 45 minutes or until puffs are firm in the center. Serve immediately.

Serves 6.

Photograph by Vince Lupo

*O*ne thing about spending time in my "crab lab" is—it's work, work, work, test, test, test, and taste, taste, taste!

CAMBRIDGE CRAB SALAD IN RING MOLD

🦀 *Looking for a menu for that next luncheon or late evening supper? Plan the meal around a salad. All you need to add is bread, a beverage, and a luscious dessert.*

1   tablespoon unflavored gelatin
¼   cup cold water
1   can (8 ounces) tomato sauce
2   packages (3 ounces each) cream cheese
1   teaspoon grated onion
½   cup chopped celery
½   cup diced cucumber
¼   teaspoon salt
    dash of cayenne pepper
1   pound crabmeat
    salad greens
    mayonnaise

Soften gelatin in cold water for 5 minutes. Heat tomato sauce to boiling; add gelatin and stir until dissolved. Chill until almost congealed. Soften cream cheese at room temperature. Add onion, celery, cucumber, salt, cayenne pepper, and crabmeat; fold into gelatin mixture. Place in a 1-quart ring mold and chill until firm. Unmold on salad greens; garnish with mayonnaise.

Serves 6.

Little did I know, when I was talking on the telephone with Dana Austin Lawhorne, that this doodle would become a page in this book. Thanks, Dana!

CRABMEAT WITH AVOCADO WHITEHALL

🦀 *This rich and satisfying crab salad is simply sensational. It teams lump crabmeat with tender, buttery avocado in a light dressing—all topped with crunchy walnuts.*

DRESSING:
- ¼ cup lemon juice
- 2 dashes aromatic bitters
-    salt and pepper to taste
- ½ cup olive oil

SALAD MEDLEY:
- 3 medium tomatoes, thinly sliced
- 12 black olives, pitted
- 2 ripe avocados, thinly sliced
-    juice of 1 lemon
- 1 pound lump crabmeat
- 6 button mushrooms, sliced
- ½ cup chopped English walnuts

Dressing: Whisk the lemon juice and aromatic bitters with salt and pepper and add the olive oil.

Salad medley: Toss the tomatoes and olives with half of the dressing and arrange them around the edges of eight plates. Arrange the sliced avocados within the circle, leaving space in the center for the crabmeat. Sprinkle the avocados with lemon juice. Toss the crabmeat and mushrooms with the remaining dressing and mound onto the middle of each plate. Top with chopped English walnuts.

Serves 8.

Cantler's Riverside Inn, on Mill Creek in Annapolis, Maryland, has earned its reputation as one of the top crab houses of the Chesapeake region. While walking their docks, I noticed this sign and quickly snapped this photo.

COBBS CREEK BAKED CRAB

Every summer during my childhood, we looked forward to Sunday dinners. This was the time that family members gathered around the picnic table in the side yard and feasted on tasty baked crab casseroles. Just biting into this light and fluffy delight takes me back to those enchanting times.

1	**pound crabmeat**
1⅓	**cups chopped celery**
1	**cup mayonnaise**
½	**cup chopped onion**
⅓	**cup chopped green pepper**
1	**teaspoon Worcestershire sauce**
½	**teaspoon salt**
½	**cup soft breadcrumbs**
½	**cup grated sharp cheddar cheese**

Combine crabmeat, celery, mayonnaise, onion, green pepper, Worcestershire sauce and salt. Place this mixture in a buttered 2-quart casserole. Combine breadcrumbs and cheese; sprinkle over the top of the crab mixture. Bake at 350°F for 25 to 30 minutes or until thoroughly heated and crumbs are lightly browned.

Serves 6.

I came across this sign while driving through Smithfield, Virginia. I prayed that Sunday—for family, friends, and steamed crabs.

TILGHMAN ISLAND ELEGANT CRAB CASSEROLE

One-pot meals and hearty casseroles are the order of the day in many Tilghman Island kitchens. This recipe, which is a cross between a delicate pudding and a casserole, is perfect for a Sunday supper or for those times when the whole family is at home.

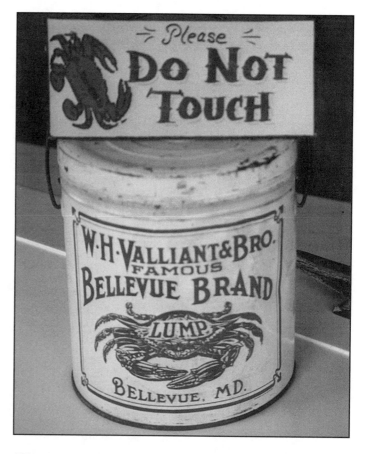

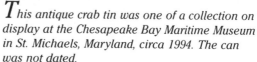

2   cans (10 ounces each) cut asparagus
      spears, drained
1   pound crabmeat
1   cup sliced almonds
½   cup chopped celery
½   cup mayonnaise
2   tablespoons lemon juice
¾   cup grated sharp cheddar cheese
      paprika

Place asparagus in a buttered baking dish approximately 12 x 8 x 2 inches. Combine crabmeat, almonds, celery, mayonnaise and lemon juice. Spread crab mixture over asparagus. Top with cheese. Sprinkle with paprika. Bake at 400°F for 15 to 20 minutes or until heated thoroughly and cheese is melted.

Serves 6.

This antique crab tin was one of a collection on display at the Chesapeake Bay Maritime Museum in St. Michaels, Maryland, circa 1994. The can was not dated.

63

DONNA'S OWN CRAB CAKES

🦀 *This recipe is from Donna Stewart of Baltimore, Maryland. Donna explains that the addition of a beaten egg white gives these crab cakes just enough to help hold the patties together for easy frying.*

1   egg white, beaten until stiff
1   heaping tablespoon mayonnaise
1   heaping teaspoon Dijon mustard
1   teaspoon Worcestershire sauce
2   teaspoons Old Bay seasoning
2   dashes Tabasco sauce
1   slice bread
1   pound backfin crabmeat
    paprika

Add mayonnaise, mustard, Worcestershire sauce, Old Bay seasoning, and Tabasco sauce to the beaten egg white. Grate bread into this mixture. Stir with a spoon and then gently fold in the crabmeat. Form into cakes on a buttered baking sheet. Sprinkle cakes with paprika. Broil in oven 5 to 6 minutes until tops are golden brown.

Serves 6.

*D*riving on Route 40 near Essex, Maryland, I saw this sign leaning against a produce stand. The crab cakes weren't much, but what can you expect for a dollar each? Try Donna's instead!

64

CHESAPEAKE CITY CRAB SOUP

🦀 *A roux is a mixture of flour and fat that, after being slowly cooked over low heat, is used to thicken soups and sauces. There are three classic roux: white, blond and brown. The color and flavor are determined by how long the roux cooks.*

ROUX:

1	medium onion, minced
4	cloves garlic, minced
4	tablespoons butter
3	tablespoons all-purpose flour
1½	teaspoons pepper
½	teaspoon salt
1	tablespoon dry mustard
	dash of cayenne pepper
½	teaspoon Old Bay seasoning

SOUP:

1	quart cream
1	pound crabmeat
3	tablespoons sherry
	chopped fresh parsley

Roux: Sauté onion and garlic in butter; when onion is golden, add flour, pepper, salt, dry mustard, cayenne pepper, and Old Bay. Make a blond roux, being careful not to overcook.

Soup: When the roux is ready, add cream, stir and bring just to a boil. Add crabmeat and bring back to a boil. Immediately add sherry and remove from heat. Adjust salt and pepper. Ladle into bowls and sprinkle with parsley. Serve with additional sherry for those who like a bit more.

Serves 6.

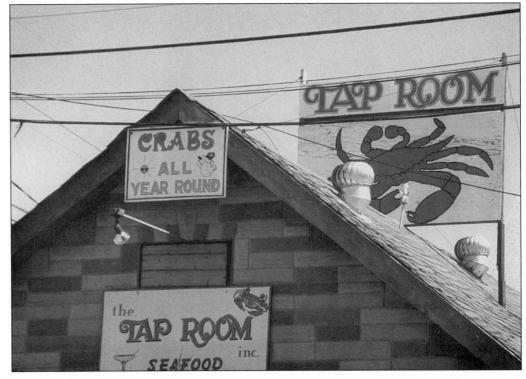

Chesapeake City, Maryland, is near the "Peake" of the Chesapeake Bay. The town came into existence because of the Chesapeake & Delaware Canal that links Chesapeake Bay across the Delmarva Peninsula. Another reason for its fame is that it is home to the Tap Room, famous for its steamed crabs and ice cold beer.

DEAN GORE'S HOT CRAB PIE

🦀 *With a busy schedule like Dean has, it's almost impossible for him to take the time to prepare a full course meal. He says, "I like this hot crab pie. I toss everything into a bowl, cover it with cheese, lay out some crackers, and open a bottle of wine. Now, that's living!"*

1   **pound crabmeat**
2   **tablespoons capers, drained**
2   **tablespoons minced green onion**
1   **teaspoon lemon juice**
3   **dashes Tabasco sauce**
1   **cup mayonnaise**
1   **cup grated sharp cheese**
    crackers

Combine crabmeat, capers, green onion, lemon juice, Tabasco sauce, and mayonnaise. Put the mixture in a buttered 10-inch pie pan and cover with the cheese. Bake at 350°F for 25 minutes or until bubbling. Serve hot with crackers.
    Serves 6 to 8.

*T*alking to an old-timer one day, he said, "I remember when crabs sold for fifty cents a dozen. Why nowadays some places want a dollar each." I wonder what he would say if he saw this sign? I snapped this photo at Cantler's Riverside Inn, Annapolis, Maryland, in 1996.

TOM VERNON'S 3-PEPPER CRAB BAKE

🦀 *A crab bake is one of the premier dishes of Chesapeake cookery, and this recipe from Tom Vernon does the dish proud. Tom likes to paint with his food, and red, green and yellow peppers add flair to this creative dish. He sometimes adds an Imperial topping made with 1 egg, ¼ cup mayonnaise, a pinch of paprika and about a teaspoon of parsley combined in a small bowl and mixed well.*

1	pound crabmeat
¼	cup chopped celery
¼	cup chopped red pepper
¼	cup chopped yellow pepper
¼	cup chopped green pepper
½	cup chopped onion
1	cup mayonnaise
1	teaspoon Worcestershire sauce
½	teaspoon salt
½	cup soft breadcrumbs
¼	cup grated sharp cheddar cheese

Combine crabmeat, celery, peppers, onion, mayonnaise, Worcestershire sauce and salt. Place mixture in a buttered 2-quart casserole. Combine breadcrumbs and cheese; sprinkle over top of crab mixture. Bake at 350°F for 25 to 30 minutes or until thoroughly heated and crumbs are light golden brown.

Serves 6.

I spotted this sign at Smithfield Station, along the Pagan River in Smithfield, Virginia. This restaurant is the perfect place to watch the sun descend on the river, and also the perfect place to enjoy Chesapeake cooking at its finest.

BOHEMIA RIVER CRAB STEW

Approaching the head of the Chesapeake Bay, and about five miles up the Elk River, the Bohemia River comes in from the east. As a river, it's a rather small affair, but what it lacks in size it makes up for in beauty. I've heard many boaters say it's one of the most beautiful three-mile stretches in all of Bay Country.

1   **stick butter**
1   **leek, chopped (white parts only)**
1   **onion, chopped**
3   **ribs celery, chopped**
2   **tablespoons all-purpose flour**
1   **teaspoon tomato paste**
1   **teaspoon dry oregano**
1   **quart chicken broth**
1   **quart fish stock**
4   **ounces crab roe**
1   **pound crabmeat**
4   **tablespoons sherry**
1   **teaspoon Worcestershire sauce**
    salt and pepper to taste
2   **egg yolks, beaten**
½   **pint cream**

Melt butter in a saucepan; add leek, onion and celery and simmer until tender. Add flour, tomato paste and oregano; stir well.

Stir in chicken broth and fish stock, then boil for 30 minutes, stirring occasionally. Add crab roe, crabmeat, sherry, Worcestershire sauce, salt and pepper. Cook for 5 minutes, then remove from heat. Add egg yolks and cream. Serve at once.

Serves 12.

"Sooks" are egg-bearing female crabs. You'll know when you see one, because a sook has a large orange egg mass on her underbelly. If you have trouble obtaining crab roe while preparing this recipe, substitute finely chopped carrots.

MUDDY CREEK BOURRIDE (BOO-REED)

🦀 *A bourride is similar to a bouillabaisse. This fish soup is pungent with garlic, onion, orange peel and saffron. It is thickened with egg yolks and can be flavored with* aioli. *I like to serve it with roasted garlic bread. (Cut the top off a head of garlic, top it with olive oil and fresh herbs, and bake it for an hour at 350°—then spread the roasted garlic on bread.)*

1   **live lobster**
3   **large crabs**
4   **quarts fish stock**
1   **rockfish, dressed and boned**
1   **pound shrimp, shelled and deveined**
1   **pound bay scallops, halved**
¼   **cup olive oil**
1   **large carrot, minced**
1   **large Vidalia onion, sliced**
2   **large leeks, sliced (white part only)**
3   **large cloves garlic, minced**
3   **large ripe tomatoes, peeled and**
      chopped
½   **cup sherry**
1   **bouquet garni**
2   **1-inch pieces orange rind, minced**
1   **teaspoon ground saffron**
1   **pound fresh green beans, chopped**
      salt to taste

Drop live lobster into boiling salted water and cook until it turns red; reserve cooking liquid. Shell crabs and lobster body, leaving legs and claws whole; refrigerate until ready to use. Add fish stock to reserved lobster cooking liquid, adding more water if necessary to make 6 quarts. Bring to a boil, reduce heat, and simmer until stock is reduced by one-fourth. Strain through a double thickness of cheesecloth; reserve. Pour oil into a Dutch oven large enough to hold all the seafood and stock. Over low heat, cook carrot, onion, leeks, and garlic just until tender. Add remaining ingredients and simmer for about 15 minutes to allow flavors to marry.

Bring to a boil, add all the seafood except the lobster, and cook for about 8 minutes, or until shrimp are pink and scallops tender. Do not overcook. Add lobster pieces and cook only to heat through. Remove bouquet garni. Serve with garlic bread and chilled Chardonnay.

Serves 8 to 10.

A bouquet garni is a bunch of herbs (the classic trio being parsley, thyme and bay leaf) that are either tied together or placed in a cheesecloth bag and used to flavor soups, stews and broths. The bag is removed before the dish is served.

CARTER CREEK HOT CRAB BREAD

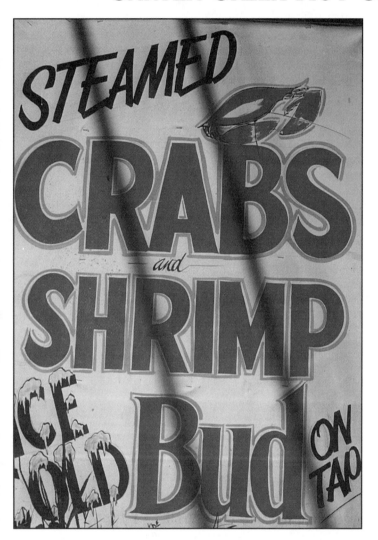

🦀 *It's high summer in Bay Country. The living is easy and the fish are jumping. The time is now for filling up on crabs, fish and the other bounties from Chesapeake waterways. A great appetizer to begin your bay adventure is this hot crab bread.*

1	**pound crabmeat**
½	**cup mayonnaise**
½	**cup sour cream**
2	**tablespoons chopped fresh parsley**
1	**tablespoon lemon juice**
2	**garlic cloves, minced**
1	**loaf Italian bread**
2	**tablespoons butter**
½	**pound sliced Jarlsberg cheese**

Combine crabmeat, mayonnaise, sour cream, parsley, lemon juice and garlic and chill for one hour. Slice bread in half lengthwise and spread with butter. Arrange cheese slices on bottom half of bread. Top with crab mixture. Cover with top half of bread, wrap in foil and bake at 350°F for 25 minutes. Cut into slices to serve.

Serves about 20.

Someone once said, "a picture is worth a thousand words." There are only two words I want to hear: "Let's eat!"

RAYMOND MCALWEE'S CRAB CASSEROLE

🦀 *You will note that I've not added any salt to this recipe. That means you'll have to find something else that does what salt does, which is to bring out the natural flavor in foods. Fortunately, there are four very good natural flavor enhancers: parsley, celery, wine, and lemon. Experiment and find the one that works best for your tastebuds. Raymond McAlwee suggests that you try parsley. If you do, add it at the end of the cooking process.*

1   **small red pepper, chopped**
3   **ribs celery, chopped**
1   **small onion, chopped**
2   **teaspoons butter**
¾   **pound Ritz crackers, crushed**

1   **pound crabmeat**
3   **hard-boiled eggs, sliced thin**
1   **tablespoon chopped parsley**
1   **can (10¾ ounces) mushroom soup**
1   **cup milk**

Sauté pepper, celery, and onion in butter, but do not brown. Butter a baking dish and cover the bottom with one-half the Ritz cracker crumbs. Layer with crabmeat, sautéed vegetables and hard-cooked eggs. Add parsley. Dilute mushroom soup with milk and pour over. Cover with a layer of cracker crumbs. Bake at 350°F until bubbly, approximately 25 minutes.
Serves 6.

I snapped this sign hung in the stairway at a crab house— as if someone might forget. I know Raymond won't and I know I won't.

JUG BAY CRAB TARTS

🦀 *Very simply, a tart is a pastry crust with shallow sides, a filling, and no top crust. The filling can be sweet (fruit or sweet custard) or savory (meat, cheese or crab and vegetables).*

tart pastry for 8 individual tarts
2 **tablespoons oil**
¼ **cup unsalted butter**
3 **leeks, sliced (white part only)**
6 **shallots, minced**
½ **cup peeled, seeded and chopped ripe tomatoes**
20 **green olives, pitted and chopped**
1 **pound crabmeat**
3 **eggs, separated**
1 **cup chicken stock**
juice of 1 lemon
¼ **pound Parmigiano-Reggiano cheese, grated**
sliced leeks for garnish

Line eight 1-cup tart pans with pastry, crimp the edges, and prick bottoms with a fork. Press foil into the pastry, fill with dried beans, and bake in a preheated 400°F oven for 8 minutes, or until pastry is light brown. Let cool.

In a large skillet, heat oil and butter and sauté leeks and shallots until translucent. Add tomatoes and sauté until mixture is soft. Stir in olives and crabmeat; set aside. In a large bowl, beat egg yolks, chicken stock, lemon juice, and cheese until smooth. Stir in the crab and leek mixture. In a separate bowl, beat egg whites until they form stiff peaks and gently fold into crab mixture. Spoon into the tart shells. Return tart pans to the 400°F oven and bake for 10 to 15 minutes, or until filling is puffed and golden brown.

Serves 8.

*W*hen I snapped this photo at Crosby Crab Co., Manassas, Virginia, circa 1980, gas was selling at $1.22⁹ and crabs were selling at $3.99 a dozen. As of this writing, gas is $1.03⁹ and crabs are $22.00 a dozen!

CRAB LOVERS' COMPANION SALAD

🦀 *Watercress is a close relative of the nasturtium and is cultivated for its roundish, crisp, dark green, rather peppery-tasting leaves. I find that it's best to wash it and shake it dry just before using. And if you really want to impress dinner guests, garnish their salad plates with freshly picked nasturtium blossoms! Colorful and tasty!*

SALAD:
- 4 **cups romaine lettuce torn into bite-size pieces**
- 1½ **cups watercress**
- 1 **small papaya, peeled and sliced**
- 1 **pound lump crabmeat**
- 1 **can (6 ounces) marinated artichoke hearts, drained**

COMPANION DRESSING:
- ½ **cup mayonnaise**
- 2 **tablespoons chili sauce**
- 1 **teaspoon lemon juice**
- 2 **drops Angostura bitters**
- ¼ **cup heavy cream**

Salad: Divide romaine pieces among four salad plates. Remove leaves of watercress and pile them on top of the romaine. Place the papaya on top of the watercress, mound the crabmeat in the center, and circle with artichoke hearts. Serve with Companion Dressing.

Companion Dressing: Mix all ingredients except heavy cream. Just before serving, whip cream and fold into the dressing mixture.

Serves 4.

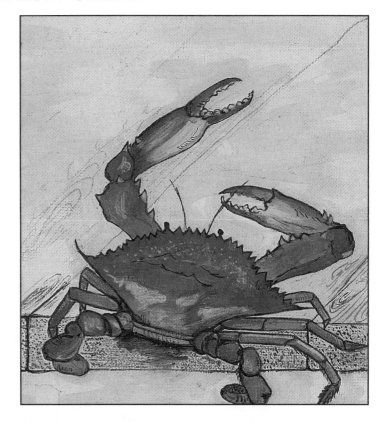

*T*his illustration is another of my telephone conversation doodles. Did you know that crabs have been caught and eaten since long before recorded history? Commercial crabbing as a significant industry, however, didn't start in the Chesapeake Bay until the late 1870s, and the first recorded shipment of soft-shell crabs was from Crisfield, Maryland, to Philadelphia, Pennsylvania, sometime around 1873.

CHILLED AVOCADO SOUP WITH LUMP CRAB

🦀 *The Romans believed that fresh dill was a symbol of good luck. This annual herb grows to a height of about three feet and has feathery green leaves called* dill weed. *The distinctive flavor of fresh dill weed is in no way translated to its dried form, so use only fresh dill in this delightful soup and bring nothing but good luck to your guests.*

1   **large ripe avocado, peeled and pitted**
1   **cup heavy cream**
1   **teaspoon grated onion**
½   **teaspoon salt**
    pinch of cayenne pepper
4   **cups chicken broth**
8   **ounces lump crabmeat**
    snipped dill weed

Force avocado through a coarse sieve into a bowl. In a food processor fitted with a steel blade or in a blender in batches, combine the avocado, cream, onion, salt and cayenne pepper.

Add chicken broth in a stream and blend the soup until smooth. Transfer to a bowl and chill for 3 hours. Ladle into chilled bowls, add crabmeat, and garnish each serving with 1 teaspoon snipped dill weed.

Serves 6.

There aren't many crab houses and seafood markets around the Chesapeake that I haven't visited. As I travel, I always look for one thing: the crab sign! This sign tells me that I'm going to have a delightful dinner. Care to join me?

CRAB CROSTINI VESPUCCI

🦀 Crostini *means "little toast" in Italian. Crostini are small slices of toasted bread, usually brushed with olive oil. The word also describes canapes made by topping small slices of toast with a savory topping. For a great appetizer, simply cut bread into small rounds, toast them, and top with this savory crab mixture.*

8 ounces lump crabmeat
¼ cup diced red bell pepper
3 tablespoons mayonnaise
1 teaspoon chopped garlic
2 tablespoons chopped fresh parsley
1 tablespoon chopped fresh chives
1 tablespoon fresh lemon juice
1 tablespoon Dijon mustard
¼ cup grated Parmigiano-Reggiano cheese
4 drops hot pepper sauce
1 loaf Italian bread, cut into 16 slices

In a bowl, combine the crabmeat, red bell pepper, mayonnaise, garlic, parsley, chives, lemon juice, mustard, Parmigiano-Reggiano cheese, and hot pepper sauce; blend well. Spread crab mixture on each slice of bread. Place the bread slices on a broiler pan and broil 4 inches from the heat for 5 to 6 minutes, or until lightly browned.
Serves 8.

The best steamed crabs are those just pulled from the Bay and popped into the pot. The crabs pictured here were prepared for me by the gang at Wehrs Crab House on Kent Island in Chester, Maryland. Three of these beauties is all it took to prepare this recipe.

EASTERN SHORE CRAB FRITTERS

🦀 *You can have New York and all its glitter.*
Just give me the shore and a tasty crab fritter.

2¼   cups all-purpose flour
1½   cups warm water
¼   cup vegetable oil
1   teaspoon chopped garlic
½   teaspoon salt
½   teaspoon black pepper
2   tablespoons Old Bay seasoning
1   pound backfin crabmeat
½   cup chopped scallions
½   cup diced Smithfield ham
3   egg whites, beaten until stiff
    peanut oil for frying
    Cocktail Sauce (recipe below)

In a small bowl, whisk together flour, water, and oil. Combine with garlic, salt, pepper, and Old Bay seasoning. Gently add crabmeat, scallions, and ham and mix with a spoon. Fold in egg whites. Drop by large spoonfuls into peanut oil. Fry on both sides until firm. Drain. Serve immediately with cocktail sauce.
Serves 8 to 10.

COCKTAIL SAUCE:
1   cup ketchup
2   tablespoons horseradish
4   teaspoons lemon juice
2   tablespoons Worcestershire sauce
⅛   teaspoon Tabasco sauce

Combine ingredients and mix. Store in refrigerator until ready to use.

The Bible states, "Man does not live by bread alone." He also needs crab fritters and oyster fritters!

CHAPTER 4
Crabba-Dabba-Do

Photograph by A. Aubrey Bodine, Mariners Museum, Newport News, VA

CRAB CAKES DELMARVA

🦀 *Chet Andrew Libertini of Columbia, Maryland, shares with us his recipe for Eastern Shore crab cakes. Try them with his Old Bayonnaise. It's original and it's good.*

1   extra large egg
1   tablespoon mayonnaise
2   tablespoons Old Bay seasoning
1   tablespoon prepared yellow mustard
1   tablespoon Worcestershire sauce
1   teaspoon lemon juice
    dash of hot sauce
1   tablespoon chopped fresh parsley
4   individual saltine crackers, crushed
1   pound lump crabmeat

Beat egg with mayonnaise and Old Bay seasoning, yellow mustard, Worcestershire sauce, lemon juice, hot sauce and parsley. Crush the soda crackers well and add.

Fold crabmeat into the wet mixture gently. Form six round crab cakes. Broil for 7-9 minutes or until brown. Serve with Old Bayonnaise.

Serves 6.

OLD BAYONNAISE:
3   tablespoons mayonnaise
1   teaspoon Dijon mustard
⅛   teaspoon Old Bay seasoning

Mix all ingredients.

George D. Spence & Sons proudly celebrates the Bicentennial in 1976 on the east side of the Machipongo River, the only river on the Eastern Shore of Virginia.

CRAB CRÊPES WITH CREAM SAUCE

These light, paper-thin creations are smooth-textured, lightly flavored and highly nutritious, and the crabmeat filling adds to the great balance of tastes. Garnish with chive blossoms to make a perfect presentation.

CRÊPES:
- ½ cup milk
- ½ cup water
- 2 large eggs
- ½ teaspoon salt
- 1 tablespoon salad oil
- ¾ cup instant flour
- Cream Sauce (recipe follows)
- salad oil

In a small bowl, whip together milk, water, eggs, salt and oil; beat in flour. Let batter stand 1 hour. Heat a 6-inch fry pan and grease lightly with salad oil. Pour in just enough batter to cover the pan with a very thin layer (about 2 tablespoons), tilting pan to spread batter evenly. Cook on one side, turn with a spatula and brown the other side. Cook the crêpes one by one, stacking them between pieces of wax paper, until 12 crêpes have been made.

Spread cream sauce on each crêpe (approximately 3 tablespoons), roll up and put in a shallow baking pan. Brush tops with salad oil.

Bake at 350°F until well heated, about 20 minutes. Heat remaining cream sauce and serve over crêpes.

Serves six, 2 crêpes each.

CREAM SAUCE:
- 4 tablespoons butter
- 2 tablespoons all-purpose flour
- 2 tablespoons chopped white mushrooms
- 1 cup milk
- 1 teaspoon sherry
- 8 ounces crabmeat

Melt butter, stir in flour and mushrooms, and add milk and sherry. Cook, stirring, until smooth and thick. Fold in crabmeat gently.

"I sit alone and weep for the misery of the world that does not have blue crabs and a Jersey cow. . . ."

—Marjorie Kinnan Rawlings
Cross Creek

79

CAPE CHARLES SHELLFISH STEW

🦀 *Cape Charles, a tiny town on Virginia's lower Eastern Shore, was named for the nearby Cape at the entrance to the Chesapeake Bay. This shellfish stew gained in popularity because of the abundance of blue crabs harvested here and the fresh shrimp harvested just south of the Bay's mouth.*

6 tablespoons butter
½ cup chopped onion
½ cup chopped celery
2 cups fish stock
1 cup diced tomatoes with juices
1½ cups tomato juice
2 tablespoons dry sherry
¼ cup pearl barley
2 bay leaves
1 tablespoon Worcestershire sauce
1 tablespoon Old Bay seasoning
1 teaspoon dried oregano
½ teaspoon chopped garlic
½ teaspoon Tabasco sauce
pinch of cayenne pepper
1 pound uncooked medium shrimp, shelled and deveined
8 ounces crabmeat
salt and pepper
½ cup chopped fresh basil for garnish

Melt butter in a large saucepan over medium-high heat. Add onion and celery; sauté until tender, about 5 minutes. Add fish stock, tomatoes with their juices, tomato juice and sherry. Bring to a boil. Add barley, bay leaves, Worcestershire sauce, Old Bay seasoning, oregano, garlic powder, Tabasco sauce and cayenne pepper and simmer until the barley is tender, about 25 minutes.

Add shrimp and crabmeat; simmer until shrimp are cooked through, about 3 minutes. Season with salt and pepper. Garnish with fresh basil.

Serves 6.

Photograph by Susan Glaser

I always thought pearl barley was an early jazz singing sensation, but I guess I was mistaken. In researching this recipe, I found that pearl barley is actually a grain that has had the bran removed and has been steamed and polished. It is used in stews like this as a thickener.

CRAB LINGUINE CAKES WITH CILANTRO-LIME SAUCE

🦀 *The term "pasta" is used broadly to describe a wide variety of noodles. There are hundreds of shapes, sizes, thicknesses and colors of pasta. Feel free to experiment and use your favorite. The results will be rewarding. This recipe works well with linguine or spaghetti.*

- 1 **cup cooked linguine**
- 2 **eggs, beaten**
- 3 **green onions, finely chopped**
- ¼ **cup fine dry breadcrumbs**
- 2 **tablespoons snipped fresh cilantro**
- 2 **tablespoons chopped green pepper**
- 2 **teaspoons olive oil**
- ¼ **teaspoon salt**
- ¼ **teaspoon pepper**
- 8 **ounces lump crabmeat**
- 2 **tablespoons oil for frying**
  Cilantro-Lime Sauce (recipe follows)
  lime wedges

Chop the cooked linguine into small pieces. Set aside. In a large mixing bowl, combine the eggs, green onion, breadcrumbs, cilantro, green pepper, olive oil, salt, and pepper. Add crabmeat; mix well. Add the chopped linguine and mix again. Using about 2 tablespoons of mixture for each crab cake, shape into 12 patties about ½ inch thick. In a large, heavy skillet, heat the 2 tablespoons frying oil. Over medium heat, cook the patties, a few at a time, about 3 minutes on each side or until golden brown. Drain on paper towels. Keep covered in a warm oven while preparing remaining cakes. Serve the crab cakes warm with Cilantro-Lime Sauce and lime wedges.
Serves 12.

CILANTRO-LIME SAUCE:
- ¼ **cup mayonnaise**
- 1 **tablespoon fresh cilantro, finely snipped**
- ½ **lime peel, finely shredded**
- 1 **tablespoon fresh lime juice**

Mix together, cover and chill until serving time.
Makes ½ cup.

*W*hat attracted me first to this roadside tavern was the balloons swaying in the breeze. Chaney's Restaurant, in North Beach, Maryland, had a unique way to get me inside—when I noticed that the bottom half of the phone number was cut off the crab sign, I just had to go inside and check it out. You guessed it—another dozen, lickety split.

81

BALTIMORE CRAB BALLS

🦀 *Appetizers tempt and seduce the palate, preparing it for the next course. A good appetizer should complement, not compete, with the rest of the meal, so plan carefully. Appetizers are versatile—many can be doubled to serve as a main course for lunch, dinner or brunch, and some work as party finger foods or garnishes for other dishes. These crab balls are like that.*

4 tablespoons butter
1 teaspoon salt
$\frac{1}{8}$ teaspoon cayenne pepper
$\frac{1}{8}$ teaspoon mace
$\frac{1}{8}$ teaspoon nutmeg
1 teaspoon mustard
$\frac{1}{2}$ cup soft breadcrumbs
1 pound crabmeat
2 egg yolks, beaten
 flour for dredging
 oil for deep frying

Melt butter, add salt, cayenne pepper, mace, nutmeg, mustard and breadcrumbs. Mix in crabmeat and beaten egg yolks. Refrigerate until firm. Then roll into small balls, dredge with flour, and fry in hot oil to a nice golden brown.

Makes 2 to 4 dozen crab balls depending on size.

For years the Fat Crab Restaurant sat on the banks of the West River in Galesville, Maryland. It was a popular spot for steamed crabs and for the Wednesday night sailboat races. Sadly, it went south and all that remains is this crab logo and good memories.

CRAB NORFOLK IN PUFF PASTRY

🦀 *Puff pastry is a feathery, many-layered French invention made by rolling and folding chilled butter into a simple dough so that the dough separates into tissue-thin "leaves" when baked. Look for it in the frozen food section of your grocery store and follow the package directions carefully.*

4	**ounces lump crabmeat**
2	**artichoke hearts, sliced**
2	**ounces prosciutto, diced**
4	**tablespoons clarified butter**
1	**teaspoon sherry**
½	**cup light cream**
	salt and pepper
	fresh parsley
	puff pastry

Sauté crabmeat, artichoke hearts, and prosciutto in the butter over medium heat for 1 minute. Add sherry and cream and reduce by half. Season to taste with salt and pepper. Add parsley for garnish.

Serve in puff pastry.

This photograph by A. Aubrey Bodine shows steam rising from the cookers of a crab–picking house on Virginia's Northern Neck.

Photograph by A. Aubrey Bodine, Mariners Museum, Newport News, VA

NOMINI CREEK CRAB SOUFFLÉ

🦀 *In French,* soufflé *means, literally, "puffed up." When you fold beaten egg whites into a soufflé batter, fold in one fourth of the whites first, then very lightly fold in the remainder in a gentle over and over motion so air remains in the whites after they've been combined with the batter.*

3	tablespoons butter
3	tablespoons all-purpose flour
¼	cup milk
2	egg yolks
½	teaspoon salt
1	tablespoon minced fresh chives
1	tablespoon minced fresh parsley
½	teaspoon dried savory
1-2	dashes Tabasco sauce
⅔	cup grated cheddar cheese
2	tablespoon Madeira
1	pound crabmeat
1	teaspoon lemon juice
1	tablespoon butter, softened
5	egg whites
⅓	cup grated Parmigiano-Reggiano cheese

Melt butter in a saucepan over low heat, then stir in flour, keeping the mixture lump-free. Let bubble for about 1 minute, then remove from heat and stir in milk with a wire whisk, mixing briskly. Return to heat and keep stirring constantly until sauce thickens to a pastelike consistency. Remove from heat and beat in egg yolks, one at a time, then add salt, chives, parsley, savory, Tabasco sauce, cheddar cheese, and the Madeira. Let cool.

Sprinkle crabmeat with lemon juice and set aside. Butter 4 scallop shells. Beat egg whites until they form stiff peaks, then fold into cooled sauce. Put a spoonful of soufflé mixture into each shell, then gently place one-quarter of the crabmeat in each one. Divide the remaining soufflé mixture among the shells, mounding neatly on top, but do not let them overflow. Sprinkle with Parmigiano-Reggiano cheese.

Preheat oven to 425°F. Bake for 10 minutes; reduce heat to 375°F and bake for 10 minutes more.

Serves 4.

While driving through a residential neighborhood in Forestville, Maryland, I noticed an old school bus that had been converted into a place to cook and sell steamed crabs. Of course, I had to stop and buy a dozen. That's when I noticed the stenciling near the bus windows!

CRAB PERRY CABIN

🦀 *The surprise ingredient in this recipe is the water chestnuts. The edible tuber of a water plant indigenous to southeast Asia, its flesh is white, crunchy and juicy. The flavor is bland with a hint of sweetness.*

    5   tablespoons butter
    1   cup sliced fresh mushrooms
    1   cup finely chopped celery
    1   pound lump crabmeat
   ¼   cup sliced water chestnuts
    3   large ripe avocados
        lemon juice
    1   cup heavy cream
    1   tablespoon Dijon mustard
    1   teaspoon Worcestershire sauce
   ½   teaspoon sugar
    3   drops Tabasco sauce
    1   cup mayonnaise
        juice of ½ lime
        salt to taste
   ½   cup slivered blanched almonds,
          toasted, plus additional for garnish
    2   tablespoons chopped fresh parsley
    1   tablespoon brandy
        lemon and lime slices for garnish

In a skillet, melt 2 tablespoon of the butter, add mushrooms and celery, and sauté for about 5 minutes, stirring occasionally. Add crabmeat and water chestnuts. Stir until ingredients are well mixed. Cook, covered, over low heat for about 5 minutes.

Halve avocados lengthwise. Peel, discard pits and rub cut surfaces with lemon juice. Place avocados in a baking dish with ½ inch of hot water and heat in a 400°F oven for 10 minutes.

In a large saucepan, combine the remaining 3 tablespoons butter, the heavy cream, mustard, Worcestershire sauce, sugar, Tabasco sauce, and mayonnaise. Heat to almost boiling, stirring constantly. Stir in lime juice and salt. Add crabmeat mixture and blanched almonds; mix well. Stir in parsley and brandy. Remove avocados to a serving dish. Fill with the hot crabmeat mixture and top with additional toasted almonds. Garnish with lemon and lime slices.

Serves 6.

Crabs, yes! That's all it took. There I was driving down Belair Road in northeast Baltimore, Maryland, and the urge for crabs struck. You never know when it's going to happen—it just does. I pulled in and went inside. My waitress said, "We're glad you stopped. Did you know that Paul Newman eats J.C.'s crabs?" So does Whitey Schmidt!

GREEN CRAB SOUP

I should have been a pair of ragged claws, scuttling across the floor of silent seas.

T.S. ELIOT

3 cups green pea soup
4 cups chicken stock
1 pound crabmeat
¼ cup white rum
   salt and freshly ground black pepper
2 cups heavy cream, whipped
   chive blossoms for garnish

Mix green pea soup and stock in a saucepan. Cook until boiling, about 4 minutes, stirring constantly. Mix in the crabmeat, the white rum, salt and pepper to taste, and cook for 5 minutes, stir-ring constantly. Fold in the whipped cream, heat thoroughly, but do not boil. Pour into warm bowls and garnish with chive blossoms.

While driving north on Route 13, I noticed this fried crabs sign. I pulled in to find Metompkin Seafood. I asked about the "fried crabs" and they said, "Oh, we've had that sign up a long time, but we never sold any, so we took them off the menu." I chose instead the oyster sandwich, and it was one of the best I'd ever eaten. See how flexible I am?

CRABULOUS BAKED CRAB DIP WITH ROASTED GREAT MD GARLIC

🦀 *Glorious garlic—next to crab it's my favorite food. Various cooking methods alter its flavor substantially. Slowly baking a bulb of garlic will reduce the pungency to a soft, mellow, sweet flavor. Recipe note: If Great Maryland or elephant garlic is not available, use about 6 cloves of a smaller variety.*

- 2 **packages (8-ounces each) cream cheese**
- 3 **large cloves Great Maryland garlic, roasted***
- 1 **pound crabmeat**
- ½ **pint sour cream**
- 4 **tablespoons mayonnaise**
  juice of ½ lemon
- 2 **teaspoons Worcestershire sauce**
- 1 **teaspoon dry mustard**
- ½ **cup grated cheddar cheese, divided**

Soften cream cheese to room temperature. Add garlic, crabmeat, sour cream, mayonnaise, lemon juice, Worcestershire sauce, dry mustard and half of the cheddar cheese. Put in a baking dish and sprinkle the remaining cheese on top. Bake at 350°F for 45 to 50 minutes.

Serve with Crusty Crustacean Bread (see page 89).

*To roast garlic: Place garlic on a sheet of aluminum foil. Sprinkle with olive oil and a dash each of salt and pepper. Gather up the foil to cover the garlic and bake for about 45 minutes at 350°F. Cool at room temperature, peel and mash.

*C*rabs, corn and cantaloupe characterize the lifestyle of the colorful people who live and work in the Upper Bay crab country. The warmth and friendliness of the people are evident for those who linger long enough to find out. I photographed this fieldside sign near Rock Hall, Maryland around 1983.

CRAB HOUSE CREAM OF CRAB SOUP

🦀 *If the bisque turns out too thick for your liking, a little milk can be added to thin out the consistency. If, on the other hand, the soup turns out too thin for your tastes, simply uncover the pot and simmer the soup base 15 minutes or so longer.*

2   quarts half-and-half
2   quarts heavy whipping cream
¼   cup Minor's chicken base
¼   cup dry sherry
    pinch of white pepper
1   teaspoon Old Bay seasoning
½   pound butter
1   cup all-purpose flour
1   medium carrot, shredded
1½ pounds lump crabmeat

Heat half-and-half and whipping cream slowly in large pot for about 40 minutes to 165° to 175°F. Add chicken base, sherry and white pepper and Old Bay seasoning and continue heating to 180°F. Make a roux by melting butter and adding flour, stirring until mixture is about as thick as oatmeal. Add the roux to the hot cream mixture. Stir to thicken, about 10 minutes. Sprinkle carrot into the soup. Add crabmeat and heat, but don't boil. Serve soup with additional sherry.

Serves 12.

*T*his photograph shows a crab picker weighing up another pound of fresh Maryland lump crabmeat. I know what I'm having for dinner!

Photograph by Vince Lupo

CRUSTY CRUSTACEAN BREAD

🦀 *I started out one morning to make the perfect roll for crab cake sandwiches, but I knew the minute I finished kneading the dough that it was too heavy. So I simply turned my error into this wonderful bread, a pleasure for the eye as well as the palate. It has traveled around the world and has been featured on Maryland Public Television.*

½ **cup warm water (105°F to 115°F)**
2 **packages active dry yeast**
¾ **cup warm milk (105°F to 115°F)**
¼ **cup sugar**
3 **tablespoons butter**
2 **teaspoons salt**
4¾ **to 5¼ cups all-purpose flour**
3 **eggs**
2 **strips lemon peel, about 2 inches long**
2 **raisins**

Place warm water in a large, warm bowl. Sprinkle in yeast; stir until dissolved. Add warm milk, sugar, butter, salt, and 2 cups flour; blend well. Stir in 2 eggs and enough of the remaining flour to make a soft dough. Knead on a lightly floured surface until smooth and elastic, 4 to 6 minutes. Place in a greased bowl, turning to grease top. Cover; let rise in warm, draft-free place until doubled in size, 30 to 45 minutes.

Punch dough down. Remove it to a lightly floured surface and follow these steps, using the photograph as a guide:

1. Divide dough in half and set one half aside.

2. Divide the other half into 12 balls of equal size.

3. Use 8 of the balls to make crab legs.

4. Combine 2 balls to make one crab claw and the last 2 to make the other claw.

5. Use the other half of the dough to shape the crab body.

6. Assemble the crab on a large baking sheet by pinching the legs onto the body. Use raisins and lemon peel to make eyes and antennae.

Cover with a towel and let rise in a warm, draft-free place until doubled in size, 20 to 40 minutes.

7. Lightly beat the remaining egg; brush on the crab. Bake at 400°F for 15 minutes. If too dark after 10 minutes of baking, cover with a tent of aluminum foil. Remove from oven, and after 10 minutes, remove from baking sheet and let cool on a wire rack.

Serves a crowd.

*K*neading yeast dough is one of the most rewarding steps of bread making. You get your hands on the dough, and you feel it develop and change. There's a sense of accomplishment and pride as the dough takes shape.

DAD'S CRAB CAKES

🦀 *Cherry Barranco of Milton, Delaware won first prize at the Coast Day 1997 Crab Cake Cook-off sponsored by the University of Delaware Sea Grant Program. Dad will be proud.*

2	**pounds crabmeat**
2	**eggs**
1	**teaspoon lemon juice**
½	**cup mayonnaise**
¼	**cup mustard**
1	**small onion, finely chopped**
1	**green pepper, finely chopped**
1	**cup crushed saltine crackers**
1	**teaspoon Tabasco sauce**
2	**teaspoons Worcestershire sauce**
1½	**teaspoons Old Bay seasoning**
1	**tablespoon chopped fresh parsley**
	dash of garlic powder
	olive oil for frying

Combine all ingredients except oil in a large bowl, mixing well. Form into cakes and refrigerate. Broil in oven or fry in olive oil until golden brown. Serve with fresh salsa or your favorite condiments.

Serves 12.

"The kind of crabbing my wife likes to do is to return from an afternoon's swim or sunbathing session, open the refrigerator door, and find a generous plate of Crab Cakes all ready to cook."
— *Euell Gibbons,* Stalking the Wild Asparagus

CRAB WITH MACADAMIA NUTS & CREAM SAUCE

Macadamia nuts have come into their own! Their crisp, creamy texture and appealingly delicate flavor have made them such favorites that clever cooks everywhere are finding new uses for them. See what I mean in this casserole.

4	tablespoons butter
2	tablespoons flour
1	cup milk
1	pound crabmeat
½	teaspoon salt
½	teaspoon paprika
2	tablespoons chopped parsley
1	tablespoon lemon juice
¾	cup macadamia nuts, ground

Melt butter, stir in flour, and add milk. Cook, stirring, until smooth and thick. Add salt, paprika, parsley, lemon juice, and crabmeat. Fill casserole and sprinkle with macadamia nuts. Bake at 350°F until nuts are golden brown, about 25 to 30 minutes.

Serves 4.

There's no single correct method of eating a crab, but rather schools of thought. There are neat pickers, who first pick their crabs clean, then eat the meat in a glorious succession of mouthfuls . . . then there are those who slurp and gobble as they pick. Some even pick with a fork! Some people use mallets to break open the claws, and others use knife handles. Some people use knives to dismantle the crab and others rely on their fingers. It's purely a matter of choice!

CRABMEAT GARNHAM

🦀 *For the toast rounds in this recipe, I find it far better to make my own than use store-bought bread. The day before you plan to make this dish, make a cylindrical loaf of bread. Then slice the bread into ½-inch rounds.*

2	cloves garlic, chopped
4	tablespoons butter
⅓	cup chopped green onion
¼	cup chopped green pepper
2	teaspoons all-purpose flour
½	cup light cream
1	pound crabmeat
½	cup 2-day-old breadcrumbs
¼	cup sherry
	salt and pepper to taste
6	5-inch toast rounds
	freshly grated Parmigiano-Reggiano cheese

In a skillet, sauté garlic in butter over moderately high heat for 3 minutes and add green onion and green pepper. Reduce the heat to moderately low and cook the mixture, stirring, for 10 minutes, or until the vegetables are softened. Stir in flour and cook for 3 minutes. Add cream and cook the mixture over moderate heat, stirring, for 5 minutes, or until it is slightly thickened. Stir in crabmeat, breadcrumbs, sherry and salt and pepper. Mound this mixture on toast rounds and sprinkle each serving with 1 tablespoon Parmigiano-Reggiano cheese. Put under a broiler about 4 inches from the heat for 5 minutes, until golden brown.

Serves 6.

Anyone who has been around a basket of live crabs for more than a minute knows it pays to have a pair of gloves readily available to handle these feisty crustaceans. And anyone who has been around those Schmidt kids knows it pays to paint your name on those gloves to prove ownership!

Highway Church Crab Cakes

🦀 *This recipe is designed for people who prepare crab dishes in large quantities.*

- **6**   **sticks butter (1½ pounds)**
- **¾**   **quart chopped onion**
- **24** **pounds crabmeat**
- **3**   **quarts breadcrumbs**
- **2**   **dozen eggs, well-beaten**
- **¼**   **cup dry mustard**
- **½**   **cup seafood seasoning**
- **4**   **tablespoons salt**
- **2**   **tablespoons pepper**
- **1**   **pound flour for dredging**
     peanut oil for frying

Melt butter, add onions, and cook until tender and light brown. Mix crabmeat, onions, breadcrumbs, eggs and seasonings. Form into small cakes and roll in flour. Fry in peanut oil heated to 375°F for 2 or 3 minutes or until browned. Drain on absorbent paper and serve immediately.

Serves 50. (Two 5-ounce crab cakes each.)

Brownie's Tavern, Balto. MD

*C*rab Crack

" . . . The blue crabs come to the brown pond's edge to browse for food where the shallows are warm and small life thrives subaqueously while we approach from the airy side, great creatures bred in trees and armed with nets on poles of such length as to outreach the sideways tiptoe lurch when in a dark splash from above the crabs discover themselves to be prey." JOHN UPDIKE

93

ELIZABETH RIVER CRAB TOAST

"And one who observes a Crab among the mossy ledges and will praise and admire him for his cunning art." —Oppian, Halieutica II

8	ounces lump crabmeat
½	cup diced red bell pepper
3	tablespoons mayonnaise
2	tablespoons chopped fresh parsley
1	tablespoon chopped fresh chives
1	tablespoon fresh lime juice
1	tablespoon Dijon mustard
3	teaspoons grated Parmigiano-Reggiano cheese
4	drops Tabasco sauce
6	ounces Italian bread, cut into 16 slices

Preheat the broiler. Line a broiler pan with foil. In a medium bowl, combine the crabmeat, bell pepper, mayonnaise, parsley, chives, lime juice, mustard, Parmesan cheese, and Tabasco sauce, and blend well. Spread the crab mixture on each slice of bread. Place the bread on the broiler pan and broil 4 inches from the heat for 5 to 6 minutes, or until lightly browned.

Serves 8.

*T*here is no more fun or challenging way to catch crabs than with a hand line. This takes skill and dexterity, a keen eye, and a fast hand. For the first-time crabber, here's how it goes: You fasten a piece of bait to a long string, toss it into the waters where crabs are known to be, and wait for one to tug on the line. You pull the line in slowly and scoop the crab into the net as soon as it comes into sight.

WARE RIVER CRAB À LA BO HERRMAN

Serve this spicy dish with steamed white rice or hot buttered noodles. It only takes about 15 minutes to make!

2 tablespoons olive oil
1 small onion, chopped
1 garlic clove, minced
1 cup unsweetened coconut milk
1 teaspoon lime zest
2 tablespoons fresh lime juice
¼ teaspoon salt
½ teaspoon crushed hot red pepper
1 tablespoon peanut butter
8 ounces crabmeat
1 tablespoon chopped cilantro

In a large skillet, heat olive oil over medium-high heat until hot. Add onion and garlic and cook, stirring often, until softened, about 3 minutes. Pour in coconut milk, lime zest, lime juice, salt, and hot pepper. Raise heat to high and boil, stirring constantly, until reduced slightly, about 1 minute.

Add peanut butter, reduce heat to low, and cook, stirring until thickened, about 1 minute. Stir in crabmeat and cook, stirring constantly, until warmed through, 1 to 2 minutes. Serve hot, garnished with chopped cilantro.

Serves 4.

After 20-plus years of taking photographs of everything crabby, it's sometimes difficult to recall where a certain picture was taken. This shot of Cindy's Seafood is one of those. If you know where it is, drop me a postcard! Thanks.

SPICY CRAB WONTONS

🦀 *Wontons are a chinese specialty similar to Italian ravioli. These bite-size dough pillows take on a new energy when filled with a spicy mixture of crabmeat, cream cheese and seasonings. Most wontons can be boiled or steamed, but this recipe is best when deep fried. Serve them as an appetizer, snack or side dish—and they adapt well to a number of sauces.*

8	ounces crabmeat
1	pound cream cheese, softened
¼	teaspoon dried thyme
1	teaspoon hot pepper sauce
2	teaspoons Worcestershire sauce
1	teaspoon white pepper
½	teaspoon salt
½	teaspoon paprika
¼	teaspoon cayenne pepper
1	clove garlic, chopped
1	package (8 ounces) wonton wrappers
	peanut oil for deep frying

In a medium bowl, combine crabmeat, cream cheese, thyme, hot pepper sauce, Worcestershire sauce, white pepper, salt, paprika, cayenne pepper, and garlic. Stir to blend.

Working with one wonton wrapper at a time, lay wrapper flat on a work surface. Place 1 teaspoon crab mixture in center and fold one corner of wrapper diagonally over filling to meet opposite corner. Moisten edges with water and press down lightly to seal. Moisten two side corners with water and bring together in center, overlapping slightly. Press with fingertips to seal tightly. Place on a large baking sheet and cover with a damp cloth to prevent drying out. Continue until all wrappers are filled.

Deep fry in batches for 1 minute until golden brown. Drain on paper towels.

Serves 8.

Throngs of people stop at roadside fruit and vegetable stands on summer weekends. The sight of deep red tomatoes, glossy green peppers and a sign that reads "Hot Steamed Crabs to Go" is enough to start me thinking about dinner!

FOG POINT FONDUE

🦀 *You don't have to own a fondue pot to prepare this recipe. Just heat the mixture in a double boiler and either serve from that or transfer the contents to a chafing dish.*

½ **pound cream cheese**
1½ **cups grated Gruyere cheese**
½ **cup milk**
¼ **teaspoon lemon pepper**
   salt and freshly ground pepper to taste
¼ **cup sherry**
1 **pound crabmeat**
   french bread, cut into 1½-inch cubes

In a fondue pot set over low heat, combine cheeses, milk, lemon pepper, salt and pepper, and sherry. Stir until blended and smooth. Add crabmeat and heat, stirring occasionally, for 5 to 10 minutes, or until hot and bubbly. For serving, spear cubes of bread with a fondue fork and swirl in figure-eight motion. If fondue thickens on standing, stir in a little additional milk or sherry.
   Serves 8 to 10.

*H*ere's another photograph of a crab truck. I spotted it in a parking lot somewhere off Route 2 in Pasadena, Maryland. I called to get more information, but the number had been disconnected.

FRIED CRABS WITH GRAVY

🦀 *The Maryland Seafood Festival is held in Annapolis the first full weekend in September each year. About ten years ago I met Mike and Eva Pinder there. It didn't take long for our conversation to lead to fried crabs with gravy, and they thoughtfully offered to share their recipe—so here it is!*

1   **dozen fresh crabs**
9   **strips of bacon, diced**
    all-purpose flour for dredging
½   **teaspoon cayenne pepper**
⅛   **teaspoon celery seed**
    salt and crab seasoning to taste

While they're still alive, pull off claws and top shells of crabs. Discard fins, apron and devil fingers. Scrape the insides from the body cavity into a bowl and reserve. In a large, deep frying pan, fry bacon pieces until done, and remove.

Roll crabs and claws in flour, place into hot bacon fat, brown on both sides, and remove.

Place the scraped insides into a blender or processor to liquefy. Add enough flour to the bacon fat to brown and make a smooth, thick roux. Add enough water to half fill pan and stir to remove lumps. Then add the liquefied insides, bacon pieces, cayenne pepper, celery seed, salt and crab seasoning and stir. Place crabs and claws into gravy, making sure they are covered. Cover the pot, turn down heat to a simmer, and cook for 1 to 1½ hours, stirring from time to time to keep from sticking. If gravy is too thick, thin with water. If not thick enough, stir in a semi-thick paste of flour and water. Use gravy on rice or noodles. Corn on the cob goes great with this.

Serves three, 4 crabs each.

During the 1980s, the House of Crabs in Ocean City, Maryland, was one of my favorite stops. I remember a sign that hung in the restaurant: "Crabs are like cars—you can buy compacts or Cadillacs. We sell Cadillacs." The guy hanging out in this photo is Chris Hopkins.

CHAPTER 5
Crab Art

Illustration by Margaret Scott

MATT'S DEVILED CRAB

 *During the 1950s, throughout southern Maryland deviled crabs appeared in every bar, cocktail lounge and bowling alley. The idea was simply to take fresh crabmeat and cook it with one or more hot ingredients such as chili pepper flakes, hot sauce or mustard. You get the idea. You can turn up the heat to satisfy your own taste.*

2   **tablespoons chopped onion**
3   **tablespoons butter**
2   **tablespoons all-purpose flour**
¾   **cup milk**
½   **teaspoon salt**
     dash of pepper
½   **teaspoon dry mustard**
1   **teaspoon Worcestershire sauce**
½   **teaspoon dried sage**
1½   **teaspoons dried thyme**
     dash of cayenne pepper
1   **tablespoon lemon juice**

1   **egg, beaten**
1   **tablespoon chopped fresh parsley**
1   **pound crab meat**
1   **tablespoon butter**
¼   **cup dry breadcrumbs**

Cook onion in butter until tender. Blend in flour. Add milk gradually and cook until thick, stirring constantly. Add salt, pepper, dry mustard, Worcestershire sauce, sage, thyme, cayenne pepper and lemon juice. Stir a little of the hot sauce into the egg; add to the remaining sauce, stirring constantly. Add parsley and crabmeat. Place in 12 buttered individual shells or custard cups. Combine butter and breadcrumbs; sprinkle over the top of each shell. Bake at 350°F for 30 minutes or until golden brown.

Serves 6.

Crab art comes in many forms, some expected, some . . . well . . . I'll never forget the day my son Matt came home and said, "Dad, I got this one for you!" Matt, you devil, you.

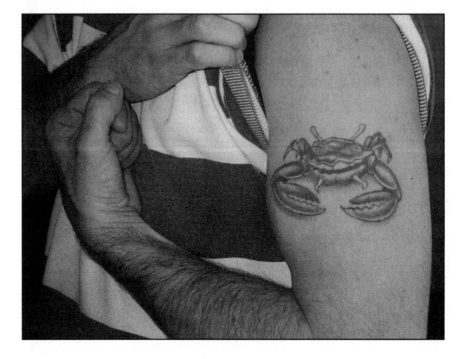

POTTS POINT CRAB CAKES

🦀 *Tartar sauce is basically a mayonnaise given piquancy by the addition of chopped capers, onions and pickles. It is served mostly with fried fish, but is excellent with crabmeat.*

½ **cup diced green pepper**
½ **cup diced red pepper**
1 **tablespoon butter**
1 **pound crabmeat**
⅓ **cup tartar sauce**
   (recipe follows)
2 **teaspoons Worcestershire sauce**
2 **teaspoons minced fresh parsley**
1 **egg**
4 **Ritz crackers, crumbled**

   salt and pepper
5⅓ **tablespoons butter for frying**
½ **cup vegetable oil for frying**

Sauté green and red peppers in one tablespoon butter until tender. Cool. In a mixing bowl, gently combine crabmeat, tartar sauce, Worcestershire sauce, parsley, egg, Ritz crackers, and salt and pepper, being careful not to overwork—you want the crabmeat to have some texture. If the mixture seems too moist, crumble in another cracker or two. Mold the mixture into patties and keep refrigerated until it's time to cook.

In a large skillet, heat butter and oil over medium heat. Fry crab cakes on each side until golden brown. Remove from pan. Serve immediately with additional tartar sauce.

Serves 4.

TARTAR SAUCE:
1 **cup mayonnaise**
½ **cup finely chopped dill pickle**
¼ **cup minced onion**
2 **tablespoons chopped fresh parsley**
1 **tablespoon dill pickle juice**

Mix all the ingredients together in a bowl. Chill for at least 1 hour before serving.

Chef Jim Wylie of Pier III Seafood House in Popes Creek, Maryland, takes great pride in his tattoos and also makes an excellent crab cake.

BUTLERS HOLE CRAB PUFFS

🦀 *The puffs and filling for this sophisticated appetizer can be prepared one day ahead. Serve the appetizers with an aperitif made from Italian sparkling wine and the juice of blood oranges. The puffs are also nice with sparkling wine alone.*

PUFFS:
- 1 **stick butter**
- 1 **cup water**
- ½ **teaspoon salt**
- 1 **cup all-purpose flour**
- 4 **large eggs**

FILLING:
- 8 **ounces crabmeat**
- ½ **cup mayonnaise**
- ½ **teaspoon sherry**
- ¼ **cup finely chopped celery**
- ½ **teaspoon curry powder**
  salt and pepper to taste

Puffs: In a medium saucepan, heat butter and water over high heat. Stir until butter is melted. When mixture begins to boil, add the salt and flour all at once. Lower the heat. Stir the mixture vigorously over low heat until completely mixed. The mixture will pull away from the sides and form a small ball. As soon as it does, remove from heat and add the eggs one at a time. Beat well after each addition until smooth and shiny. Drop by the teaspoonful 3 inches apart onto an ungreased baking sheet and shape into mounds. Bake puffs at 400°F for 30 minutes. Cool on a rack.

Filling and assembly: Mix all filling ingredients together in a bowl. Split puffs and fill with crabmeat mixture.

Makes about 4 dozen.

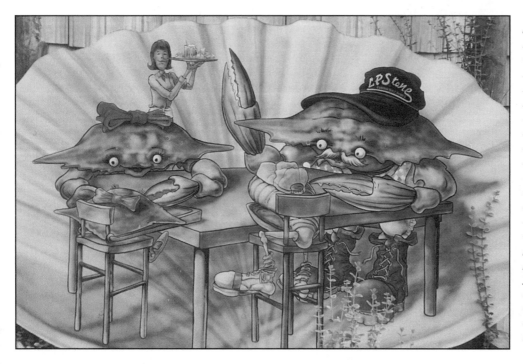

*S*toney's Seafood House on tiny Broomes Island, Maryland, is home to all sorts of steamed seafood, including a handpicked selection of fresh-caught crustaceans piled high on a platter. While you're waiting for your order, check out the artwork—it's fun!

PLEASANT POINT CASSEROLE

🦀 *This casserole is easily prepared with domestic white mushrooms, but I have tried it with lightly sautéed shiitake mushrooms (harvested just outside my back door!) with excellent results.*

1 **pound medium shrimp, shelled and deveined**
1 **package (9-ounces) frozen artichoke hearts**
4 **tablespoons butter**
½ **pound mushrooms, sliced**
2 **cloves garlic, minced**
2 **tablespoons chopped shallots**
¼ **cup all-purpose flour**
   pepper to taste
1 **tablespoon chopped fresh dill**
¾ **cup milk**
½ **cup sherry**
8 **ounces sharp cheddar cheese, grated**
1 **pound lump crabmeat**
¼ **cup grated Parmigiano-Reggiano cheese**

Cook the shrimp in a pan of boiling salted water for 2 to 3 minutes until pink. Cook artichoke hearts according to package directions. Cut each heart in half and set aside with the shrimp. Melt 2 tablespoons of the butter in a medium saucepan and sauté the mushrooms until just tender. Remove from pan and add the remaining 2 tablespoons butter, garlic, and shallots. Sauté gently for 4 minutes and remove pan from heat.

Whisk in flour, pepper and dill. Add the milk and cook, stirring constantly, until sauce thickens. Add the sherry and half the grated cheddar cheese. Gently fold the crabmeat, artichoke hearts, shrimp, mushrooms and remaining cheddar cheese into the sauce. Pour into a buttered 2-quart casserole and sprinkle with Parmigiano-Reggiano cheese. Bake for 30 minutes at 375°F or until golden brown.

Serves 8 to 10.

The J. Millard Tawes Historical Museum and Visitor Center in Crisfield, Maryland, is fast becoming one of the most visited places on Maryland's Eastern Shore. The Museum is packed with history and lore of the crab industry as well as works of art like this painting by Shirley Ennis that covers a wall in the museum.

GOLDEN BEACH CRAB CASSEROLE

🦀 *The sugar snap edible-pod pea is the best variety of "eat the whole thing" pea to use in this recipe. Be sure to harvest pods only when the peas are fully developed and round in the pods. Steaming them quickly is all that's needed.*

1	**pound crabmeat**
1	**cup chopped celery**
½	**cup chopped onion**
1	**cup freshly steamed sugar snap peapods**
2	**tablespoons chopped fresh parsley**
1	**cup mayonnaise**
1	**cup milk**
1½	**cups herb stuffing mix, plus ½ cup reserved and crushed**
1	**tablespoon butter**

Toss the crabmeat, celery, onion, peapods and parsley in a mixing bowl. Fold in the mayonnaise, milk and 1½ cups stuffing mix. Combine well and spoon into a buttered 2-quart casserole dish. Spread the ½ cup of crushed stuffing on top and dot with butter. Bake uncovered at 350°F for 30 minutes or until browned.

Serves 4.

To me there's nothing better than to sit outdoors, drink a cold beer, and polish off another dozen hot steamed crabs. The day I took this picture, I was sitting on the Island Breeze crab deck at Evan's Seafood on St. George Island, Maryland. That's when I spotted this potted geranium.

GODS GRACE POINT CRAB CASSEROLE

🦀 *Crab casseroles are one of the premier dishes of Chesapeake crab cookery. This recipe is from my sister Althea, who is affectionately known as Aunt Al and whose baking skills are legendary. This creamy dish makes a fine dinner entrée, but it's also a great change of pace for a Sunday brunch. Thanks, Al.*

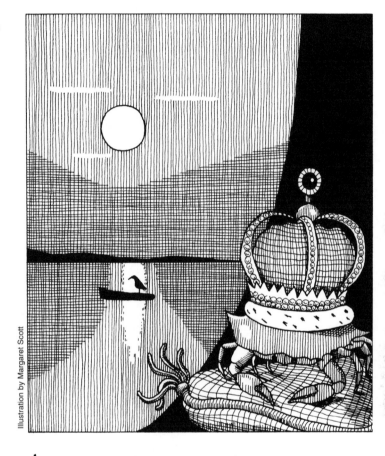

Illustration by Margaret Scott

4	**tablespoons butter**
4	**tablespoons all-purpose flour**
1	**cup milk**
1	**cup chicken stock**
½	**teaspoon curry powder**
½	**teaspoon paprika**
½	**teaspoon dry mustard**
½	**teaspoon dried basil**
2	**tablespoons minced fresh parsley**
1	**can (8-ounces) sliced mushrooms, drained**
2	**tablespoons freshly squeezed lemon juice**
⅔	**cup light cream**
	salt and pepper
1	**pound crabmeat**
½	**teaspoon grated lemon zest**
¾	**cup fresh buttered breadcrumbs**

Melt butter in a saucepan and stir in flour. Whisk in the milk and chicken stock gradually, stirring constantly over medium heat until thickened. Add the curry powder, paprika, mustard, basil, parsley, mushrooms, lemon juice and cream. Season to taste with salt and pepper and simmer for 2 to 3 minutes. Place the crabmeat in a 2-quart casserole and lightly toss with lemon zest. Pour in the sauce and fold it gently into the crabmeat. Sprinkle with buttered breadcrumbs. Bake at 350°F for 20 minutes until bubbly and golden brown.

Serves 6.

*A*s I said before, crab art comes in many forms, and one of them is poetic. I remember this poem I saw taped on the window of a crab carryout:

> *Crabs cooked at CRAB KING are really a delight.*
> *You can eat them in the morning and all through the night.*
> *Never have to worry about ever getting fat.*
> *Just buy a bag and try them and that will settle that.*

105

YORKSHIRE CRAB SOUP

🦀 *While vacationing in York, England some twenty years ago, I discovered this delightful crab soup in, of all places, a Chinese restaurant. When I saw it on the menu, I couldn't resist.*

⅓ **cup cooking oil**
5 **slices fresh ginger root about 1 inch wide**
1 **cup finely chopped onion**
1 **pound crabmeat**
½ **teaspoon salt**
2 **tablespoons sherry**
8 **cups chicken stock**
4 **egg whites**
½ **cup light cream**
1 **tablespoon cornstarch mixed with 2 tablespoons cold water**

Heat oil in a large saucepan. Add ginger and onion and sauté about 1 minute. Add crabmeat, salt, and sherry, stir lightly, and cook for about 1 minute. Add chicken stock and bring to a boil. Remove ginger root.

Beat egg whites until stiff and combine with the cream and cornstarch/water mixture. Stir gradually into the hot crab mixture. Stir constantly and let soup simmer about 3 minutes, but do not boil. Serve at once in warmed bowls. Serves 8.

This is my good friend Graham Bruce of Irvington, Virginia. Graham is a celebrated painter, author and sportsman. If you ever get to Irvington, I suggest you stop by his shop and see all the treasures he has to offer. Maybe he'll show you his prize catch and tell you how he caught it!

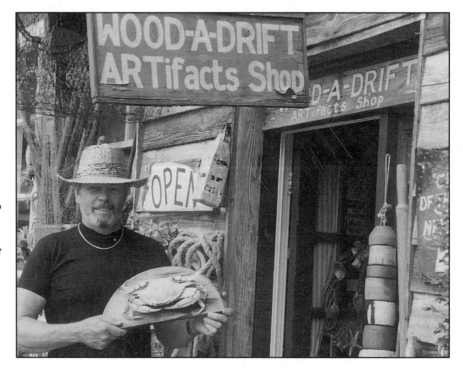

106

PEACHBLOSSOM CREEK CRAB PUFFS

🦀 *When temperatures soar and days get lazy, it's a terrific time to entertain. Invitations are casual, dress is comfortable, and there's none of the stress of more formal dinner parties. In a word, it's fun. What's also fun is watching your guests tear into these crab puffs.*

12	slices white bread
1	pound crabmeat
8	ounces Swiss cheese, shredded
⅓	cup mayonnaise
2	tablespoons sherry
1	tablespoon lemon juice
	salt
	pinch of cayenne pepper
½	teaspoon seafood seasoning
½	cup grated Parmigiano-Reggiano cheese
	paprika

Remove crusts from bread slices and cut each into quarters. Broil on a cookie sheet until lightly toasted; cool. Mix crabmeat, Swiss cheese, mayonnaise, sherry, lemon juice, salt to taste, cayenne pepper and seafood seasoning. Spoon the mixture onto the toasted sides of the bread and sprinkle lightly with Parmigiano-Reggiano cheese and paprika. To serve, bake for 10 minutes at 350°F or until light golden brown.

Makes 48 puffs.

I found this crab art outside the Pier Street Restaurant in Oxford, Maryland. Pier Street is a great spot for tasty food, and Oxford is a great place to relive a part of Maryland's historic past.

CHUCKATUCK CREEK CRABMEAT COCKTAIL

🦀 *This crab salad is mounded into grapefruit shells, providing a colorful and convenient way to serve your guests.*

COCKTAIL:
- 3 **medium ruby red grapefruit**
- 8 **ounces crabmeat**
  dash of cayenne pepper
- 2 **tablespoons white rum**
- ¾ **cup cooked asparagus tips**
- 6 **lettuce leaves**

PINK DRESSING:
- 1 **cup mayonnaise**
- ⅓ **cup chili sauce**
- 1 **tablespoon grated onion**
- 1 **tablespoon chopped parsley**
- 1 **teaspoon Worcestershire sauce**
- 2 **tablespoons freshly squeezed lemon juice**

Cocktail: Cut grapefruits in half and remove the segments with a grapefruit knife. Remove the pith from the rind, scoop shells clean and save. Collect the juice and add to the fruit. Mix the crabmeat with the grapefruit and season with cayenne pepper. Add the rum and asparagus tips and toss. Refrigerate until ready to serve.

Pink Dressing and assembly: Mix all dressing ingredients, cover and chill. Fill shells with grapefruit/crab mixture, arrange each on a lettuce leaf, and spoon Pink Dressing over the top.

Serves 6.

I snapped this picture outside a country store in Issue, Maryland, about 1980.

TILE BRIDGE CRAB CASSEROLE

🦀 *Crab Imperial (or Imperial Crab) is one of the most popular dishes in Chesapeake cookery, but regardless of what you call it, it's still a casserole. Even with lobster and artichoke hearts, it's a casserole—but oh, what a casserole!*

4	tablespoons butter
1	pound fresh mushrooms
5	tablespoons all-purpose flour
2	cups half-and-half
¼	cup sherry
2	cups mayonnaise
½	cup minced fresh parsley
1	bunch scallions, chopped
2½	cups fresh breadcrumbs
1	pound crabmeat
1	pound cooked lobster, cut into chunks
2	cans (14-ounces each) artichoke hearts, quartered
½	cup freshly grated Parmigiano-Reggiano cheese

In a large saucepan, melt the butter, add the mushrooms and sauté for 5 minutes. Stir in the flour and combine well. Add the half-and-half a little at a time, stirring constantly until sauce thickens. Add the sherry and cook for 2 minutes. Remove from heat and allow to cool. Stir in the mayonnaise, parsley, scallions and breadcrumbs. Lightly fold in the crabmeat and lobster.

Butter a 9 x 13-inch casserole dish. Layer the artichoke hearts and spread the crab and lobster mixture on top. Top with Parmigiano-Reggiano cheese and bake at 350°F for 30 to 40 minutes.

Serves 10 to 12.

I'll never forget the day. Plum Tree Wildlife Refuge near Poquoson, Virginia, was my destination. I had been on back roads for about 45 minutes and hadn't seen a car coming or going. Then I discovered Bill Forrest Seafood, and this crab art was painted on the building

HORSE LANDING CREEK CRAB COOKERY

🦀 *The Drift Inn Crab house in Oraville, Maryland, is another of the Chesapeake area's top eating spots. Just outside the back door is Horse Landing Creek, where the British uploaded their horses (hence the name), marched on Washington, D.C., and burned the Capitol.*

    8   **ounces cooked medium shrimp,**
            chopped
    1   **pound crabmeat**
    1   **green pepper, minced**
    1   **small onion, minced**
    1   **cup minced celery**
    1   **cup mayonnaise**
    1   **teaspoon Worcestershire sauce**
    1   **teaspoon chopped fresh parsley**
        salt and pepper to taste
        buttered breadcrumbs

Place shrimp and crabmeat in a bowl and combine with green pepper, onion and celery. Toss with the mayonnaise, Worcestershire sauce, parsley, salt and pepper and mix well. Spoon mixture into a 2-quart casserole. Sprinkle with buttered breadcrumbs and bake at 350°F for 30 minutes until browned.

Serves 6.

Crab art takes on yet another dimension in crab flags. They appear all over Bay Country on everything from sailboats to buildings to bars and beyond.

BATTLE CREEK CRAB LINGUINE

🦀 *Linguine is Italian for "little tongues."*
Linguine are long, narrow, flat noodles sometimes
referred to as "flat spaghetti." Serve this garlicky
dish tonight and see how many little tongues lick
the plate clean!

1	pound linguine
1	stick butter
1	cup chopped green pepper
1	cup chopped Vidalia onion
½	cup chopped mushrooms
1	pound crabmeat
½	teaspoon salt
6	garlic cloves, minced
½	teaspoon oregano
⅛	teaspoon freshly ground black pepper
1	can (16-ounces) stewed tomatoes
½	cup water
	grated Parmigiano-Reggiano cheese

Bring a large pot of water to a boil. Cook linguine according to package directions. At the same time, melt the butter in a skillet and sauté the peppers, onions and mushrooms until tender, about 3 minutes. Add the crabmeat, salt, garlic, oregano and pepper and simmer for 5 minutes. Stir in the stewed tomatoes and water. Cover and simmer 3 minutes longer. Drain the pasta and toss with the sauce in a large bowl. Serve with grated Parmigiano-Reggiano cheese.

Serves 6.

*C*rab art surfaces once more, this time on a concrete driveway in Alexandria, Virginia, around 1975.

HALLOWING POINT DEVILED EGGS

Hallowing Point, on the Patuxent River near Barstow, Maryland, is one of my favorite little spots. I have many pleasant memories of this dish, eaten along with a bottle of ice cold chardonnay. Ahh . . . what a sweet life!

1   **dozen large eggs, hard-cooked and chilled**
1   **cup mayonnaise**
2   **tablespoons freshly squeezed lemon juice**
1   **teaspoon snipped fresh dill**
½   **teaspoon salt**
    dash of black pepper
    8 ounces lump crabmeat
    fresh dill for garnish

Cut eggs in half lengthwise. Remove yolks and reserve in a covered container. Combine the mayonnaise with lemon juice, dill and pepper. Mix in the crabmeat. Fill egg halves with the crab mixture and chill lightly covered until ready to serve. Sieve the yolks into a small bowl and sprinkle a small amount over each egg half. Garnish with sprigs of dill.

Serves 12.

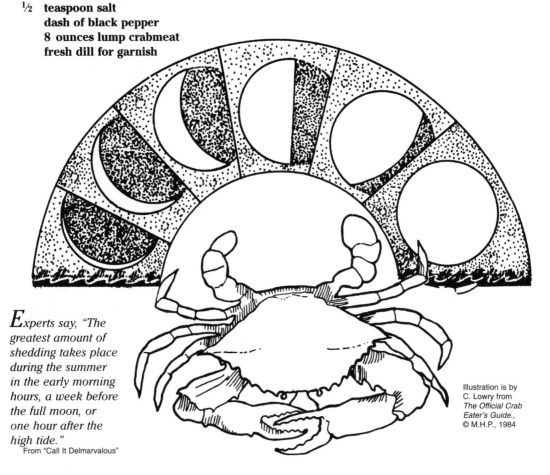

Experts say, "The greatest amount of shedding takes place during the summer in the early morning hours, a week before the full moon, or one hour after the high tide."
From "Call It Delmarvalous"

Illustration is by C. Lowry from *The Official Crab Eater's Guide.*, © M.H.P., 1984

EAGLE HARBOR SEAFOOD STEW

🦀 *Okra is the edible seedpod of a plant in the hollyhock family. The green okra pods have a ridged skin and a tapered, oblong shape. Although available fresh year-round in the South, the season for Crab Country is from about May through October. When buying fresh okra, look for firm, brightly colored pods under 4 inches long.*

2	strips bacon
2	onions, chopped
2	cloves garlic, chopped
1	green pepper, chopped
2	cans (16-ounces each) whole tomatoes
1	cup water
1	bay leaf
1	pound okra, cut in ½-inch pieces
1	tablespoon seafood seasoning
½	teaspoon cayenne pepper
1	pound medium shrimp, shelled and deveined
1	pound clams, shucked and chopped
½	pound crabmeat
½	pound striped bass fillets, chopped
	white rice

In a large pot, fry bacon until crisp. Drain and crumble. Add the onions, garlic and green pepper to the bacon drippings and fry until soft, about 5 minutes. Add the tomatoes, water, bay leaf, okra, seafood seasoning and cayenne pepper. Cook over medium heat for 15 minutes. Add shrimp, clams, crabmeat and fish fillets. Simmer for 1 hour. Serve over white rice.

Serves 12.

"Watermen say that hard crabs have more meat in them when the moon is on the wane, and that soft crabs are best and most plentiful when the moon is full . . ."

from *Chesapeake Kaleidoscope*

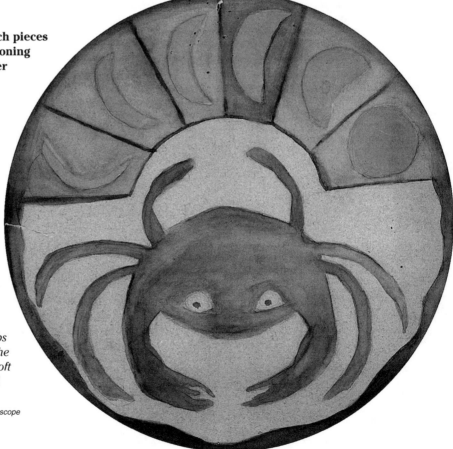

CRAB STUFFED CHICKEN BREAST

🦀 *These mouthwatering bundles are easy to prepare and are very adaptable. For instance, you can top them with fresh buffalo milk mozzarella cheese—or how about fresh basil leaves and a drizzling of olive oil? The results in either case are mighty good.*

6   chicken breasts, skinned and boned
4   tablespoons butter
½   cup chopped onion
½   cup chopped celery heart
¼   cup dry white wine
8   ounces crabmeat
½   cup cracker crumbs
½   cup all-purpose flour
1   teaspoon seafood seasoning
    salt and pepper to taste
    melted butter

Pound the chicken breasts between two sheets of waxed paper until uniform in size. In a frying pan, melt the butter and sauté the onion and celery heart until tender. Add the wine, crabmeat and cracker crumbs and combine lightly. Divide the mixture into six parts and spoon down the center of the chicken breasts. Roll each breast and tie with string. Mix flour, seafood seasoning, salt and pepper. Roll chicken in this mixture, place in a baking dish (don't crowd), and drizzle with melted butter. Bake for 45 minutes at 325°F.

Serves 6.

I found this "crabug" at Tim's Rivershore Crabhouse on the banks of the Potomac River in Dumfries, Virginia. You won't find Tim's by accident, but what you will find is wonderful Chesapeake Bay cooking. Be on the lookout for the crabug and follow it to Tim's front door.

CRABMEAT AND CUCUMBER ROUNDS

I love appetizers made of spreads on crackers or bread; dips that beg for chips, vegetables or breadsticks; and little skewers of fish or poultry. The choices are almost endless, and this kind of food makes some of the most rewarding eating I've ever experienced.

    8   **ounces crabmeat**
   ⅓   **cup mayonnaise**
   ½   **teaspoon Worcestershire sauce**
    1   **large cucumber**
         salt and pepper to taste
         sautéed toast rounds
         chopped fresh parsley

Flake crabmeat and mix with the mayonnaise, adding more mayonnaise if necessary to bind. Add Worcestershire sauce and mix well. Peel cucumber, mince, and season with salt and pepper. Spread a little cucumber on each toast round. Cover with crabmeat mixture and broil until lightly browned.

    Serves a crowd if you use small toast rounds.

I've seen crab clocks, crab pumpkins, crab flags, crabugs, crab tattoos, crab trucks, and crabby people, but this is my first crab table.

Crab table by Robert Verrier

115

SHRIMP AND CRAB IMPERIAL STEW

🦀 *Especially important to serving an appealing soup is the choice of garnish—not only for the sake of presentation, but to offer a contrasting or complementary taste to the soup.*

6	slices bacon, chopped
2	large onions, sliced
1½	quarts chicken stock
2	bags fresh spinach, rinsed and chopped
2	tomatoes, chopped
½	teaspoon grated nutmeg
	salt and pepper to taste
1	pound large shrimp, shelled and deveined
1	pound lump crabmeat
	Tabasco sauce to taste
	assorted chopped fresh herbs

Sauté bacon and sliced onion in a large pot for 5 minutes, stirring occasionally. Add stock, spinach, tomatoes, nutmeg, salt and pepper. Bring to a boil, reduce heat and cook for 15 minutes. Add the shrimp and crabmeat and cook gently until shrimp are pink, 6 to 8 minutes. Adjust seasonings and add a few dashes of Tabasco sauce to taste. Garnish with chopped fresh herbs.

Serves 12.

The Crown and Crab Tavern is on State Circle in historic Annapolis, Maryland. A step into the Treaty of Paris Restaurant is a step into the past. The restaurant's name refers to the treaty, ratified in Annapolis, that ended the Revolutionary War. You won't want to pass up this restaurant's delicious crab dishes, so keep an eye out for the Crown and Crab art.

CRAB SALAD IN CRISP ROMAINE LEAVES

Romaine's elongated head has dark green outer leaves that lighten to a delicate green in the center. The inner leaves are crisp and slightly bitter and the crunchy midrib is particularly succulent. This salad also lends itself well to Belgian endive.

	grated zest of 1 lemon
2	tablespoons lemon juice
1	teaspoon chopped fresh tarragon leaves
2	tablespoons chopped fresh garlic chives
2	tablespoons chopped fresh parsley
1	tablespoon deli-style mustard
½	cup mayonnaise
1	pound crabmeat
¾	cup diced celery
	salt, freshly ground pepper and cayenne pepper to taste
24	small romaine lettuce leaves

In a bowl, combine the lemon zest, lemon juice, tarragon leaves, garlic chives, parsley, mustard and mayonnaise; mix well. Stir in the crabmeat and celery and season with salt, pepper and cayenne. Cover and refrigerate up to 5 hours. To serve, spoon the crab mixture onto the romaine leaves and chill for at least 30 minutes to firm the filling.

Serves 8.

Trick or treat! Who says crab and pumpkin don't go together? This one received two claws-up in our annual pumpkin carving contest.

117

SHELLTOWN CRAB SANDWICHES

🦀 *Bread is so satisfying to make. There is nothing like kneading dough into a smooth and elastic mass. It can be very therapeutic—a lot of tension seems to be kneaded out as the dough takes shape. But there are times when we don't have time to bake, and if that's the case, slice open an English muffin and let the meal begin.*

1 **pound crabmeat**
1 **cup grated Gruyère cheese**
3 **tablespoons minced chives**
¼ **cup mayonnaise**
1 **tablespoon lime juice**
½ **teaspoon salt**
½ **teaspoon pepper**
3 **dashes hot pepper sauce**
2 **tablespoons butter, softened**
6 **English muffins, split**
   seafood seasoning

In a medium bowl, mix crabmeat with Gruyère cheese and chives. Stir in mayonnaise, lime juice, salt, pepper and hot sauce.

Preheat broiler. Butter English muffin halves and spread crab mixture evenly over each half. Place on a baking sheet and broil until lightly browned, 2 to 3 minutes. Serve hot, garnished with seafood seasoning.

Serves 6.

*W*hen I saw this crab truck parked in a lot in Baltimore, I couldn't let it pass by. I sat down and made this illustration—and then I went inside and guess what? I was very happy.

118

HARBOUR HOUSE CREAM OF CRAB SOUP

🦀 *The Harbour House Restaurant in downtown Annapolis was a favorite eatery for many years, like many restaurants that fall by the wayside. This recipe is too good to be forgotten, and even though it has appeared in several other cookbooks, I'm including it here.*

4 tablespoons butter
⅓ cup all-purpose flour
1 cup chicken broth
¼ teaspoon pepper
5 cups milk
1 pound crabmeat
salt to taste

Melt butter in a 3-quart pan. Blend in flour and stir until smooth. Slowly stir in chicken broth and pepper and simmer for 2 minutes, until slightly thickened. Add milk and cook slowly, stirring constantly, until thickened. Do not boil. Add crabmeat to milk mixture and salt to taste. Remove from heat and serve.

Serves 6.

Crab art takes yet another shape in this whirligig. When I saw this revolving in the wind in Baltimore around 1995, I stopped to snap a photo.

HERRING CREEK CRAB IMPERIAL

🦀 *When you are cooking with olive oil, no other ingredient you choose plays a more critical role in establishing the character of your dish. All olive oils deliver flavor and palate impressions of one kind or another. The first clue to the quality of the oil you buy is a term you must look for: "extra virgin." This means that the oil is the juice of olives obtained solely through the means of mechanical pressure—it hasn't been altered by the use of solvents of any kind.*

1   **pound crabmeat**
6   **eggs, hard-boiled**
1   **teaspoon salt**
    dash of pepper
    pinch of dry mustard
1   **tablespoon vinegar**
1   **teaspoon olive oil**
1   **tablespoon butter plus additional for**
       dotting on top of casserole
1   **tablespoon all-purpose flour**

1   **cup light cream**
1   **can (4-ounces) mushrooms, drained**
    paprika

Place crabmeat in a large bowl. Cut eggs in half, remove yolks and set aside. Chop whites and add to the crabmeat. Add salt and pepper. Mash the egg yolks. Add to them the dry mustard, the vinegar and olive oil. Mix, and add to crabmeat.

Melt the butter in a saucepan over low heat. Blend in the flour, and add cream all at once. Cook quickly, stirring constantly until mixture thickens. Pour while hot over the crab mixture. Stir together, mixing well. Add mushrooms. Place in a buttered casserole. Cover top with dots of butter and sprinkle lightly with paprika. Bake at 350°F for about 30 minutes, or until thoroughly heated and golden brown.

Serves 6 to 8.

Annapolis
SEAFOOD MARKETS
PRESENT
AIR CRAB USA®
SUPPLYING FRESH MARYLAND SEAFOOD // *TO THE ENTIRE COUNTRY*

DELIVERING
RIGHT TO THEIR DOOR
OVERNIGHT & REFRIGERATED
ANY QUANTITY OF SEAFOOD
TO ANY LITTLE TOWN THROUGHOUT THE UNITED STATES.
SEND MARYLAND CRABMEAT, OYSTERS, FISH, SOFT OR HARD CRABS,
LOBSTERS OR ANY OF OUR OVER 100 FRESH SEAFOOD PRODUCTS.

Annapolis **SEAFOOD MARKETS**
*"The Hangar of...*AIR CRAB USA*"*
CONTACT OUR AIR CARGO COORDINATOR FOR DETAILS

SEVERNA PARK   FLIGHTS LEAVE DAILY   ANNAPOLIS
544-4900   FROM RUNWAY #1   269-5380

Air Crab USA, a division of the Annapolis Seafood Markets, ships seafood anywhere in the entire country. I'm going to give them a call. I want crabs for breakfast.

CHAPTER 6
Crab Houses

Photograph by Noel Schwab

CRUSTY CREAMY MARYLAND BLUE CRAB

🦀 *Phoebe Ferguson of Crisfield, Maryland, won first prize in the main dish division at the 50th Annual Crab Cooking Contest, Crisfield, Maryland, 1997. Congratulations, Phoebe.*

FILLING:

3	tablespoons all-purpose flour
¾	tablespoon Old Bay seasoning
¼	teaspoon dry mustard
1¾	cups half-and-half
1	stick butter
⅛	teaspoon celery seed
1½	teaspoons Marsala cooking wine
1	pound crabmeat

BISCUIT CRUST:

1	package (16.3 ounces) Grands Extra Rich Biscuits

Filling: In a small bowl, blend flour, Old Bay seasoning, dry mustard, and half-and-half. Melt butter in a medium saucepan over low heat. Slowly add the flour mixture to the melted butter, stirring constantly until thick and smooth. Stir in celery seed and Marsala wine and simmer for 1 minute. Remove from heat and gently fold in crabmeat. Set aside.

Biscuit crust: On a lightly floured surface, roll one biscuit to 5½-inch diameter and place in a 6-ounce custard cup, covering the bottom and sides. Repeat until 6 cups have been lined. Fill cups with filling mixture. Cut the remaining biscuits in half and roll each to 3½-inch diameter. Lay a biscuit half on top of each custard cup, seal the edges and trim off any overlap. Bake in an oven preheated to 375°F for 20 minutes or until golden brown. Remove from cups and serve upside down.

Serves 6.

A water view is nice, but it has nothing to do with the quality of a crab house. You can't see any water at Woody's Crabhouse in North East Maryland, but you will find good crabs.

BEST EVER CRAB CAKE
(page 50)

Color insert photographs by award-winning photographer Vince Lupo.

Most yeast doughs are meant to be kneaded, shaped and patted, and your hands are just the right tools.

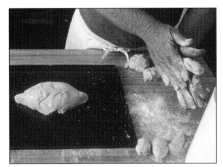

Crusty Crustacean Bread begins to take shape.

When you add the legs and claws to the crab's body, lift and pinch them into place.

Before baking, brush the bread with lightly beaten egg.

CRUSTY CRUSTACEAN BREAD
(page 89)

CRAB PICKER'S CRAB SOUP
(page 39)

BUTTERED BAKED CRAB BETTERTON
(page 13)

CRAB COVE RICE RING
(page 213)

TRAUGOTT'S SAUTÉED SOFT-SHELL CRABS
(page 40)

CRAB-STUFFED ROCKFISH
(page 49)

SHIP POINT CRAB SOUFFLÉS WITH PECANS

Velveeta was a popular food in my mother's kitchen. Hi-melt cheeses were developed to overcome the fact that processed cheese would lose flavor easily. You're going to love the flavor of these soufflés ... it can't be beat!

6	tablespoons butter
½	cup all-purpose flour
1½	cups milk, hot but not boiled
¼	teaspoon salt
	dash of pepper
	pinch of ground nutmeg
1	cup grated Velveeta cheese
4	eggs, separated
1	pound crabmeat
6	slices canned pineapple, drained
6	teaspoons toasted chopped pecans

Melt 4 tablespoons of the butter in a heavy saucepan over low heat. Stir the flour into the butter and cook slowly, stirring constantly, until well blended, about 5 minutes. Remove the pan from the heat and gradually stir in the hot milk, stirring vigorously to prevent lumping. Return to medium heat and cook, stirring constantly, until the sauce is smooth, thick, and hot. Season with salt, pepper and nutmeg. Remove from the heat and stir in the grated cheese all at once. Continue stirring until the cheese is melted. In a large bowl, beat the egg yolks until thick and lemon-colored. Slowly pour the cheese mixture into the egg yolks, stirring vigorously. Fold in the crabmeat. In a large bowl, beat the egg whites until stiff. Gently spread the cheese mixture over the egg whites and fold in until blended. Pour into six individual buttered soufflé dishes. Place the dishes in a pan filled with hot water that comes halfway up the sides and bake at 350°F until browned and a toothpick inserted gently near the center comes out clean, 45 to 55 minutes.

While the soufflés are cooking, melt the remaining butter in a heavy skillet over high heat. Add the pineapple slices and sauté on both sides until golden brown. To serve, place a pineapple slice on top of each soufflé and sprinkle with pecans.

Serves 6.

Bay Island Seafood, located at Pratt St. and Monroe in Baltimore, Maryland, can't be beat. This one makes crabs the ultimate treat!

REGISTERED TRADE MARK

"CAN'T BE BEAT"

123

SCALLOPED CRAB OYSTERSHELL POINT

The culinary world is very familiar with the distinctive flavor of the "scalloped" dishes, named for the bivalve mollusks that swim by, rapidly snapping their shells together. A single scallop shell is an ideal baking dish for a casserole like this one, made with a milk sauce and topped with breadcrumbs.

1	pound crabmeat
½	cup dry sherry
4	tablespoons butter
2	tablespoons finely chopped onion
¼	cup all-purpose flour
½	cup milk
1	cup light cream
1	tablespoon Worcestershire sauce
1	teaspoon salt
½	teaspoon pepper
2	egg yolks
2	tablespoons butter, melted
½	cup dry breadcrumbs

Sprinkle crabmeat with ¼ cup of the sherry; toss gently, but mix well. Sauté onion in 4 tablespoons butter until soft and translucent. Remove from heat and stir in flour. Gradually stir in milk and cream; bring to a boil, stirring constantly. Reduce heat and simmer until quite thick—8 to 10 minutes.

Remove from heat; add Worcestershire sauce, salt, pepper, and the rest of the sherry. Stir a little of the sauce into the egg yolks and return to the rest of the sauce in the saucepan; mix well and stir gently into the crabmeat mixture.

Turn into a lightly buttered 1-quart casserole. Toss 2 tablespoons melted butter with the breadcrumbs and sprinkle over the crabmeat. Place the casserole on a cookie sheet and bake at 350°F for 25 minutes or until bubbly and crumbs are lightly browned.

Serves 6.

FROZEN   *Christy's*   FRESH

Choice Quality

SOFT SHELL CRABS

PACKED BY
GEORGE A. CHRISTY & SON, INC.
CRISFIELD, MARYLAND

Frozen Food Permit
Md. #384

Elvis has been sighted in and around the Chesapeake Bay many times over the last 20 years. I was really surprised to see him on this box of frozen soft-shell crabs!

CHURCH CREEK CRABMEAT SPREAD

Another good use for this crabmeat spread is to simply cover flounder filets with it and then broil until the fish flakes. This is one spread that your family will want to make over and over again—and it's easy, too!

> 8   **ounces crabmeat**
> ⅓   **cup mayonnaise**
> 1   **tablespoon capers, plus additional for garnish**
>   **crackers or thinly sliced 1-inch bread rounds**
>   **snipped fresh parsley**

Mix crabmeat, mayonnaise and capers and spread on crackers or bread rounds. Sprinkle with parsley and garnish with additional capers.

Makes about 1 cup spread, enough for 4 dozen 1-inch canapés.

I snapped this photo around 1983 in Beltsville, Maryland. Between 1980 and 1985, I visited (and ate at!) more than 275 crab houses. The results? Thousands of miles, thousands of crabs, and thousands of memories.

SANDY POINT NECK CRAB BAKE

🦀 *You can fix crabs in hundreds of ways, but this has to be my favorite of 'em all . . . except for steamed, deviled, sautéed, au gratin . . .*

1½ **pounds fresh shrimp, peeled and deveined**
8 **cups water**
3 **cloves garlic, chopped**
1 **onion, quartered**
1 **bay leaf**
1 **stick butter**
1 **teaspoon lemon juice**
¾ **cup cracker crumbs**
8 **ounces crabmeat**
lemon wedges and fresh parsley for garnish

Boil shrimp in water with 1 clove garlic, onion and bay leaf for 3 minutes. Drain. Melt butter in a skillet and add remaining garlic and lemon juice. Add half of this garlic butter to the cracker crumbs. Mix well and set aside. Place shrimp and crabmeat in 4 individual casseroles, and pour remaining garlic butter evenly over top. Sprinkle with cracker crumbs and bake at 400°F for 5 minutes. Garnish with lemon wedges and parsley.
    Serves 6.

This photo I snapped along Fishing Creek in Chesapeake Beach, Maryland around 1980. At that time it was known as Jack Abbott's Crab House. Jack provided a screened porch where diners could view the active waterside life on the Creek while waiting for a tasty crab dinner.

BUY BOAT CRAB CIOPPINO

🦀 *Chesapeake Bay "buy boats" were popular around the turn of the century. These vessels held seafood bought from oyster grounds, crab rigs, tongers and dredges and rushed the fresh products to city markets immediately after purchase.*

⅓ cup olive oil
3 medium onions, chopped
1 medium green bell pepper, chopped
10 cloves garlic, minced
2 cups peeled, seeded and chopped tomatoes
¼ cup tomato paste
2 cups dry white wine
¼ cup coarsely chopped fresh Italian (flat-leaf) parsley
1 bay leaf
1 teaspoon dried oregano
½ teaspoon dried thyme
¼ cup chopped fresh basil
1 teaspoon salt
1 pound crabmeat
1 pound rockfish, cut into chunks
1 pound medium shrimp, peeled and deveined

2 dozen small clams, scrubbed
2 dozen mussels, scrubbed and debearded
additional parsley for garnish

In a large kettle, heat the olive oil, then sauté the onions, green pepper, and garlic over medium heat until soft. Add the tomatoes, tomato paste, 1 cup of the wine, the parsley, bay leaf, oregano, thyme, basil, and salt, and bring to a boil. Lower the heat and simmer 10 to 15 minutes. Add the crabmeat and chunks of fish to the pot, pushing them down into the sauce, and cook over low heat, covered, for about 10 minutes. Add the shrimp, cover again, and cook until the shrimp are pink.

In a separate pot, steam the clams and mussels in the remaining 1 cup wine (add a little water if necessary) until they open. Add the clams and mussels to the kettle. Strain the clam cooking liquid through fine cheesecloth and add it to the kettle. Garnish with parsley.

Serves 10 to 12.

Good crab houses like Gabler's Shore Restaurant near Aberdeen, Maryland, know what their customers like. The long tables are covered with brown paper, and along with the usual silverware come a wooden mallet, a paring knife, and usually a "reserved" sign, because every night the place is packed with happy crab eaters.

FAIRHAVEN FLOUNDER STUFFED WITH CRAB

🦀 *Seafood lovers will recognize quickly how good they can expect this combination to be, and indeed it is. Try it tonight!*

FLOUNDER:

8	ounces crabmeat
12	cooked shrimp
1	cup shredded Monterey jack cheese
4	large filets of flounder
1	cup dry white wine
1	cup warm Hollandaise Sauce (recipe follows)
	paprika and minced fresh parsley for garnish

HOLLANDAISE SAUCE:

1	stick butter
	juice of 1 lemon
1	tablespoon water
2	eggs
	salt and pepper

Flounder: Mix the crabmeat, shrimp and cheese together. Place ¼ of the mixture on top of each flounder filet and roll the filet around it. Secure with toothpicks and place the stuffed filets in a buttered casserole, seam side down. Pour the wine around the fish and bake until the fish flakes, 10 to 15 minutes, at 400°F.

Hollandaise Sauce: In a heavy 1-quart saucepan, melt butter. Add the lemon juice and water. In a small bowl, beat eggs with a whisk and then slowly pour into the butter-lemon mixture, stirring constantly with a whisk. As soon as the sauce begins to thicken, turn off the heat and beat until thick. Add salt and pepper to taste.

Assembly: Preheat the broiler. Remove the filets to a heatproof serving platter. Spoon the Hollandaise sauce over each filet and place under the broiler until the sauce bubbles and browns slightly, 2 to 3 minutes. Remove the toothpicks and sprinkle the filets with paprika and parsley.

Serves 4.

By now you know I'm attracted to crab art. At Gunning's Crabhouse in Baltimore, the outside crab garden is my favorite spot to sit and polish off a dozen.

ISLAND CREEK CRAB CASSEROLE

🦀 *Like many other cookery terms, "casserole" denotes both a baking dish and the food cooked in it. Casserole cooking is extremely convenient because the ingredients are cooked and served in the same dish. Notice that in this recipe, the breadcrumb topping is added for both texture and flavor.*

1 package (9-ounces) frozen artichoke hearts, cooked
1 cup grated extra-sharp cheddar cheese
2 tablespoons minced onion
4 tablespoons butter
2 tablespoons all-purpose flour
¼ teaspoon curry powder
½ teaspoon salt
1 cup milk
1 tablespoon lemon juice
1 pound crabmeat
½ cup breadcrumbs
2 tablespoons butter, melted

Place artichoke hearts in a 1-quart casserole. Sprinkle with cheese. Sauté onion in butter and add flour, curry powder and salt. Add milk and stir until sauce thickens. Add lemon juice and crabmeat and pour over artichokes. Mix breadcrumbs with melted butter and sprinkle over casserole. Bake at 350°F for 30 minutes.

Serves 6.

Solomons Crabhouse is a short distance from Island Creek and the mouth of the Patuxent River. For the many boaters cruising the Bay, it offers anchorages, marinas, an interesting maritime museum and a great place to stop and enjoy some tasty crabs.

LITTLE MONIE CREEK CRAB WENBURG

🦀 *Rich and creamy, this elegant dish may be served in patty shells made from puff pastry or over toast points.*

WENBURG:

- 2 **tablespoons butter**
- 2 **tablespoons all-purpose flour**
- ¼ **teaspoon salt**
    dash of cayenne pepper
- 1½ **cups half-and-half**
- 2 **egg yolks, beaten**
- 1 **pound crabmeat**
- 3 **tablespoons Madeira**
    paprika
    parsley sprigs

TOAST POINTS:

- 6 **slices bread**
    butter

In a saucepan, melt butter and stir in flour, salt and cayenne pepper. Add half-and-half all at once. Cook and stir until thickened and bubbly. Cook and stir 1 minute more. Stir about half of the hot mixture into the egg yolks; then pour egg yolk mixture into the hot mixture in the saucepan. Cook and stir until the mixture just boils. Reduce heat and cook, stirring constantly, for 2 more minutes. Stir in crabmeat and Madeira and heat through.

Toast points: Toast the bread, butter one side, and cut each slice into 4 small triangles.

Spoon crabmeat mixture over toast points, sprinkle with paprika, and garnish with parsley sprigs.

Serves 6.

*T*he chances of you passing up a second helping of this Crab Wenburg are about the same as me passing this sign and not stopping for a mug of beer and a cup of crab soup . . . it won't happen!

CRAB ALLEY BAY SOFT CRABS

🦀 *The use of fresh herbs does wonders for fresh soft-shell crabs. Chervil is one of the main ingredients in* fines herbes. *Though most chervil is cultivated for its leaves alone, the root is also edible and was, in fact, used by early Greeks and Romans.*

olive oil spray
2 teaspoons butter
4 cloves garlic, minced
¼ cup minced shallots
¼ cup Italian-flavored breadcrumbs
8 soft-shell crabs, cleaned, washed, patted dry
¼ teaspoon pepper
1 teaspoon minced fresh chervil
1 teaspoon minced fresh thyme
additional breadcrumbs for garnish
¼ cup minced fresh chives

Spray a non-stick frying pan with olive oil spray. Add butter, garlic and shallots and sauté over medium heat, stirring occasionally, until garlic and shallots just begin to brown. Mix in breadcrumbs, add crabs, and sauté over medium heat, turning once, until cooked. Crabs will brown when cooked. Sprinkle with pepper, chervil and thyme.

Place 2 crabs on each plate and sprinkle with more breadcrumbs and chives. Serve hot.

Serves 4.

FLY! MOTOR! SAIL!
TO...
Old Maryland Style
CRABHOUSE
AT
KENTMORR MARINA
ON
KENT ISLAND
The heart of pleasant living
5 MILES SOUTH OF BAY BRIDGE ON ROUTE 8

*K*entmorr Marina is roughly midway between the Bay Bridge and Bloody Point on Maryland's Eastern Shore, and it's one of my favorite stops when I travel the Chesapeake. Today you can feast on the restaurant's excellent steamed crabs and lump crab cakes, then play volleyball on the lawn or take windsurfing lessons on the Bay. Now you know why they call it "The Land of Pleasant Living."

CRAB MACHETTO

🦀 *Whether you prepare it for a special occasion—Thanksgiving, Christmas, New Year's—or just another weekend, this delightful dish will make your mouth run water two blocks away! It's so easy to make, anyone can do it.*

1 **pound crabmeat**
½ **cup cooked diced carrots**
1 **can cream of mushroom soup**
   dash of pepper
½ **teaspoon seafood seasoning**
½ **cup grated sharp cheese**
   paprika

Combine crabmeat, carrots, soup, pepper, and seafood seasoning. Divide among 6 buttered baking dishes. Sprinkle cheese and paprika on top of mixture. Bake at 350°F for 20 to 25 minutes or until golden brown.
   Serves 6.

It's tough to understand what happens in a new restaurant. It opens. It serves good food. But six months later it's long gone. The only thing that remains from Dunphy's is this menu cover. Thanks for the memories!

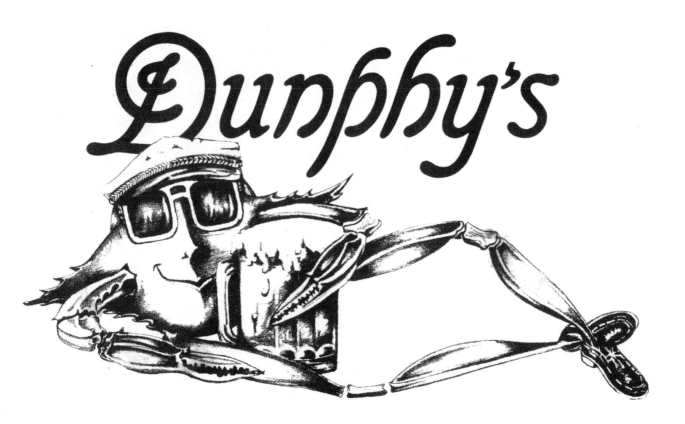

TURKEY POINT CRAB CASSEROLE

Many consider Turkey Point, at the mouth of the Elk River, to be the true "top of the Bay." Near here, the Elk, Sassafras, Susquehanna and Northeast Rivers all join forces with the Bay. Similarly, in this recipe mushrooms, crabmeat, chicken, avocados, almonds and cheese all join forces to make a delicious, healthy supper.

1	large onion, chopped
5	tablespoons butter
1	cup thinly sliced mushrooms
1	pound lump crabmeat
¾	pound chicken breasts, cooked, boned, and chopped
2	cans cream of chicken soup
½	cup chicken stock
¾	cup white wine
2	ripe avocados, peeled, seeded and diced
¾	cups slivered almonds
¾	cups grated Gruyère cheese

In a large skillet, sauté onion in butter until tender. Add mushroom slices and sauté until tender. Stir in crabmeat, chicken, chicken soup, chicken stock and wine and simmer for 5 minutes. Add the avocado. Pour the mixture into a buttered casserole. Sprinkle the top with almonds and cheese and bake at 375°F for 20 minutes.

Serves 12.

*T*he menu at Woody's reads: "We want to serve the very best crabs possible. Due to certain weather, water temperature, and tides, crab sizes and weight will vary. Our waitresses will do their very best to tell you what is available. Find out what came in today!" When a crab house provides this kind of information, you can expect the best.

HAWK'S NEST CRAB BENEDICT

🦀 *The most popular legend of the origin of Eggs Benedict says that it was first served at Manhattan's famous Delmonico's restaurant. We took their classic recipe and crowned it with crab, and it's magnificent—try it!*

DUTCH SAUCE:
- 1 **stick butter**
- 3 **egg yolks, beaten**
- 1 **tablespoon water**
- 1 **tablespoon lemon juice**
- **dash of salt**
- **dash of white pepper**

EGGS, MUFFINS AND CRABMEAT:
- 4 **eggs**
- 2 **English muffins, split**
- 8 **ounces lump crabmeat**
- **paprika**

Dutch Sauce: Cut the butter into thirds and bring it to room temperature. In the top of a double boiler, combine egg yolks, water, lemon juice, salt and pepper. Add a piece of the butter. Place over boiling water (the upper pan should not touch the water). Cook, stirring rapidly with a whisk, until butter melts and sauce begins to thicken. Add the remaining butter, a piece at a time, stirring constantly until melted. Continue to cook and stir until the sauce thickens (about 2 minutes more). Immediately remove from heat.

Eggs Benedict: Lightly grease a medium skillet. Add water to half-fill the skillet. Bring water to boiling and then reduce to a simmer (bubbles should begin to break the surface of the water). Break *one* of the eggs into a measuring cup. Carefully slide it into the simmering water, holding the lip of the cup as close to the water as possible. Repeat with the remaining eggs, allowing each egg an equal amount of space in the pan.

Simmer the eggs uncovered for 3 to 5 minutes or until the whites are completely set and yolks begin to thicken but are not hard. Remove the poached eggs with a slotted spoon and place them in a large pan of warm water to keep warm.

Place English muffin halves, cut sides up, on a baking sheet. Broil 3 to 4 inches from the heat about 1 minute or until toasted. Top each muffin half with crabmeat and broil about 1 minute more or until crabmeat is heated through. Top each muffin half with an egg; spoon Dutch Sauce over the eggs and sprinkle with paprika.

Serves 4.

*E*very good crab house should have a hand sink conveniently close to the eating area—also plenty of hand towels. A really good crab house will have two sinks!

BROOKLYN CRAB CASSEROLE

🦀 *Mom Schmidt was known for her ability to stretch a recipe, especially when she didn't know how many were coming to dinner. At the last minute, she could top this dish with four more slices of bread and four more slices of cheese.*

8   slices white bread
     butter
8   slices American cheese
1   pound crabmeat
½   pound fresh mushrooms, sliced and
       sautéed in butter
1   onion, chopped
4   eggs, beaten
2½   cups milk
½   teaspoon seafood seasoning
1   teaspoon dry mustard
1   teaspoon salt

Remove crusts from bread and butter both sides of each slice. Put 4 slices in the bottom of an 8-inch square pan. Top with 4 slices of cheese, then crabmeat, mushrooms and onion. Top onion layer with remaining cheese and end with remaining bread. Combine eggs, milk, seafood seasoning, mustard and salt. Pour over casserole, cover, and allow to stand for several hours in the refrigerator. Bake uncovered at 350°F for 60 minutes.

Serves 8.

Little did I know when I took this photograph that it would appear on a book cover and in magazine stories across the country. Circa 1980, Baltimore, Maryland.

CRAB AND CITRUS COCKTAIL WITH HERB SAUCE

🦀 *Citrus and crab work beautifully together in salads. Combining large lump crab and ruby or star grapefruit adds color to your plates, and topping it all with a delicate herb sauce it brings smiles to your guests.*

HERB SAUCE:
- ½ **cup mayonnaise**
- ½ **cup sour cream**
- 2 **tablespoons finely chopped sweet pickle**
- 1 **tablespoon sliced green onion**
- 1 **tablespoon minced fresh parsley**
- ½ **teaspoon dry mustard**
- ½ **teaspoon paprika**
- ¼ **teaspoon salt**
  - **pepper to taste**

COCKTAIL:
- 1 **pound lump crabmeat**
- 1 **orange, peeled and sectioned**
- 1 **pink grapefruit, peeled and sectioned lettuce leaves**

Herb Sauce: Combine all ingredients. Cover and chill.

Cocktail: Combine crabmeat and fruit sections. Divide mixture among 8 lettuce-lined cocktail cups. Spoon herb sauce over each.

Serves 8.

I found this crab art at Ernie's Original Crab House in Alexandria, Virginia around 1985. This restaurant is owned by the Pak family. Stop by for their tasty crabs.

(all our crabs walk sideways)

CRAB OVER ANGEL HAIR PASTA

When you cook pasta, always use plenty of boiling water so the pasta can move freely in the pot. One-half pound of noodles will require at least two quarts of water. Here are some more pasta tips: Use one teaspoon salt for each quart water, and don't break long strands of pasta— instead, lower them slowly into the boiling water, pushing them down as the ends soften.

1   package (8 ounces) angel hair pasta
    salted water
2   tablespoons butter
¼   cup olive oil
½   cup sliced green onions
1   clove garlic, minced
2   medium-size ripe tomatoes, peeled,
        seeded and chopped
¼   cup dry white wine
1   tablespoon lemon juice
8   ounces crabmeat
¼   cup chopped fresh parsley
    salt and pepper

Cook pasta in a large kettle of boiling salted water until *al dente.* Drain well and place on a warm platter; keep warm. Meanwhile, in a skillet over medium heat, place butter and oil. When butter is melted, add green onions, garlic, tomatoes, and wine. Cook, stirring, until mixture boils. Adjust heat so mixture boils gently, and cook for 2 minutes. Mix in lemon juice, crabmeat, and parsley. Cook, stirring, just until crabmeat is heated through. Season to taste with salt and pepper. Serve over pasta.

Serves 4.

Cover art by Yardley

A visit to Obrycki's in 1967 resulted in one of the best crab meals I had ever eaten. I can't remember the price of a dozen crabs back then, but I do know that a Beefeater's martini cost only a dollar!

CRABMEAT WEST RIVER

🦀 *Parmigiano-Reggiano cheese is highly nutritious and full-flavored. It delights the most exacting connoisseur as a fine table cheese, but when eaten along with crabmeat, it's magical.*

2   packages (10-ounces each) frozen
     chopped spinach, thawed
3   tablespoons butter
1   tablespoon minced onion
1   teaspoon lemon juice
½   teaspoon salt

2   tablespoons all-purpose flour
1½   cups milk
¼   cup dry sherry
½   cup grated Swiss cheese
    dash of Worcestershire sauce
    salt and pepper
1   pound crabmeat
1   cup fine dry breadcrumbs
    grated Parmigiano-Reggiano cheese
    paprika
    butter

Drain spinach and press out water. Melt 1 tablespoon of the butter in a small skillet, add onion and cook until limp. Add spinach, lemon juice and salt. Cover and cook 1 to 2 minutes, only until spinach is hot. Remove from heat and spoon into 8 ramekins. Flatten spinach out to completely cover bottoms of ramekins. Melt remaining butter in a saucepan, add flour and stir over low heat for 4 to 5 minutes. Slowly add milk and stir until thickened. Add sherry and Swiss cheese, stirring until the cheese melts. Add Worcestershire sauce and salt and pepper to taste. Remove from heat and gently add crabmeat. Spoon the mixture over the spinach. Top with breadcrumbs, Parmigiano-Reggiano, and paprika and dot with butter. Bake at 350° for 30 minutes or until thoroughly heated. Place under broiler until lightly browned.
Serves 8.

*G*ood crab houses offer wooden mallets to crack the crabs' claws. I like to use the crab knife made by Carvel Hall at Crisfield, Maryland—its heavy handle can be used to crack crab claws, so a mallet is unnecessary. If you do use a mallet, though, follow this advice: Don't smash 'em—just crack 'em.

BUSHWOOD CRAB-CANTALOUPE SALAD

'Loupes are a remarkable fruit. Around the Bay in the summertime, when the cantaloupes ripen, their fragrance fills the air. When halved and mounded with crabmeat and raspberries, the salad is intoxicating!

2	**large, ripe cantaloupes**
	lemon juice
⅓	**cup vanilla yogurt**
2	**tablespoons milk**
2	**cups chopped red raspberries**
1	**pound crabmeat**
¼	**cup chopped pecans, toasted**

Halve cantaloupes, scoop out seeds, and brush with lemon juice.

For dressing, in a medium mixing bowl, stir milk into yogurt until of desired consistency. Stir in chopped raspberries and crabmeat. Arrange cantaloupe halves on 4 salad plates. Spoon crab mixture into halves and sprinkle with pecans.

Serves 4.

This historic tavern has had as many name changes as my refrigerator door opens each day. On my last visit it appeared that time and tide were taking their downward course. It's been years since I've been back here, and I wonder what's happened to the building . . . and the sign.

HISTORIC TAVERN

COMMEMORATING THE ROLE OF TAVERNS
IN THE POLITICAL AND SOCIAL LIFE
OF OUR COUNTRY

BAILEY'S CRAB HOUSE

ESTABLISHED 1880
MR. EDWARD BAILEY, OWNER
TAVERN MONTH MAY, 1967
CITED BY
THE CARLING BREWING COMPANY AND
MARYLAND LICENSED BEVERAGE ASSOCIATION

MR. CRAB'S CRAB ACAPULCO

🦀 *Avocados are known for their lush, buttery texture and mild, faintly nutlike flavor. The flesh is usually a pale yellow-green and softly succulent. Combined with crabmeat, sherry and cheese, it produces a very pleasing taste sensation.*

4 tablespoons butter
¼ cup all-purpose flour
1⅔ cups milk
¾ teaspoon salt
1 teaspoon Worcestershire sauce
dash of seafood seasoning
2 tablespoons fresh lime juice
3 tablespoons sherry
⅓ cup grated sharp Cheddar cheese
1 pound crabmeat

4 ripe avocados
salt
toasted sesame seeds

Melt butter and blend in flour. Gradually mix in milk and cook and stir until smooth and thickened. Add salt, Worcestershire sauce, seafood seasoning, lime juice, sherry and cheese, stirring until blended. Add crabmeat and cook just until heated.

Cut avocados in half; remove seed and skin. Place in a shallow baking dish and sprinkle with salt. Heap each avocado half with crab mixture and a sprinkle of toasted sesame seeds.

Bake at 300°F for 15 minutes, just until warm. Serves 4.

I took this photograph of Mr. Crab's Sombrero while driving down Route 301 in southern Maryland around 1983. My dining experience there was unforgettable, but unfortunately you can forget going there— it closed years ago.

CRAB STUFFED PORTOBELLO MUSHROOMS

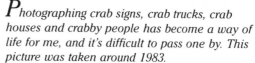*Fragrant, hot stuffed mushrooms can be an integral part of antipasto, served as a vegetable, or eaten as an entrée. Portobello mushrooms can easily measure six inches across. This recipe was designed for large mushrooms—adjust it if you buy smaller ones.*

8	**Portobello mushrooms**
8	**ounces crabmeat**
2	**ounces cream cheese**
½	**teaspoon Tabasco sauce**
2	**tablespoons chopped chives**
2	**ounces soft whole wheat breadcrumbs, buttered**

Wipe mushrooms clean; remove stems and chop fine. Combine chopped stems, crabmeat, cream cheese, Tabasco sauce and chives. Divide among mushroom caps. Sprinkle caps with breadcrumbs and place under broiler for 10 to 15 minutes until golden. Watch them—they're hot!

Serves 4.

Photographing crab signs, crab trucks, crab houses and crabby people has become a way of life for me, and it's difficult to pass one by. This picture was taken around 1983.

141

WHITEY'S RED HOT BLUE CRABS #2

🦀 *Growing up on the Chesapeake, some of my favorite childhood memories are of crab feasts. With eight brothers and five sisters, it didn't take long to learn how to dismantle a crab. When Pop Schmidt handed me an almost empty beer bottle and said "Fetch me another," I'd drain the bottle, so another memory is of how good beer tasted with crabmeat!*

½ **heaping cup seafood seasoning**
¼ **cup plus 2 tablespoons coarse salt**
3 **tablespoons red pepper**
3 **tablespoons pickling spice**
2 **tablespoons celery seed**
1 **tablespoon crushed red pepper**
12 **ounces flat beer**
    apple cider vinegar
12 **blue crabs, alive and kicking**

DIPPING SAUCE:
½ **cup apple cider vinegar**
1 **tablespoon seafood seasoning**

Combine seafood seasoning, salt, red pepper, pickling spice, celery seeds and crushed red pepper and set aside. Combine water and vinegar in equal amounts to a depth of 1 inch in a very large pot with a lid; bring to a boil. Place a rack in the pot over the boiling liquid; arrange half the crabs on the rack and sprinkle with half the seasoning mixture. Top with the remaining crabs and seasoning mixture.

Cover tightly and steam for 20 to 25 minutes, or until crabs turn bright red.

Dipping Sauce: Combine the ingredients and serve with hot or cold crabs and the beverage of your choice.

Serves 4.

Photograph by Noel Schwab

*C*aptain John's Crab House, on Cobb Island Road in southern Maryland, is one of my all-time favorite places to eat crab. Its pleasant rustic charm and unique cooking methods provide the ingredients for a delightful evening of crab dining.

CHAPTER 7
Jus' Crabbin'

Rippons Bros.
Seafo
HOOPERSVI
Phone
CATCHER
JUMBO
1
CRAB

TOMATO TORTILLA WITH CRAB 'N' CHEESE

🦀 *Start with tomato soup and serve a watercress and mixed green salad with mustard vinaigrette alongside the tortilla. Conclude with chocolate-walnut brownies.*

6	ounces grated Monterey Jack cheese
2	ounces cream cheese, softened
¼	cup chopped fresh cilantro
2	tablespoons orange juice
2	teaspoons grated orange peel
1	teaspoon grated lemon peel
	salt and pepper
8	ounces crabmeat
8	plum tomatoes, peeled, seeded and chopped
½	cup chopped green onions
1	tablespoon minced seeded jalapeño chili
8	8-inch flour tortillas
5	tablespoons vegetable oil

Mix Monterey Jack and cream cheeses, cilantro, orange juice, orange peel and lemon peel. Season mixture to taste with salt and pepper. Mix crabmeat, tomatoes, green onions and chili in a large bowl. Spread cheese mixture over half of each tortilla and top with crabmeat mixture. Fold tortillas in half and press gently to seal.

Heat 1½ tablespoons oil in each of 2 heavy, large skillets over medium heat. Working in batches, cook tortillas until cheese melts and tortillas are golden brown, about 3 minutes per side. Cut into wedges and serve.

Serves 4.

If you follow me, I know you'll end up at the water's edge with a great view of the river and a pile of hot steamed crabs skillfully prepared.

PANNED OYSTERS WITH CRABMEAT AND HAM

🦀 *The ham I use in this recipe is Smithfield ham, considered by Chesapeake chefs to be the premier country cured ham. The "Smithfield" is said to be "so loved by Queen Victoria that she had six sent to her household every week." I wonder how many pounds of crabmeat she used!*

½ **cup heavy cream**
2 **egg yolks**
   salt and pepper
5 **tablespoons butter, divided**
   1 pint oysters, drained
4 **slices bread, crust removed**
4 **wafer-thin slices country ham**
8 **ounces crabmeat**

In a bowl, whisk together the heavy cream, egg yolks and salt and pepper to taste. In a skillet, melt 1 tablespoon butter over low heat and add oysters. Cook until edges curl. Add egg yolk mixture and cook, stirring constantly, until the sauce thickens, but do not let it boil.

Toast the bread slices in an oven preheated to 300°F. Butter toasted bread and transfer to four heated plates. Trim ham slices to the size of the toast slices. In a skillet, cook ham and crabmeat in 2 tablespoons butter. Top each piece of toast with ham, then crabmeat. Spoon the panned oysters over each.

Serves 4.

Like the grinning cheshire cat in Lewis Carroll's Alice's Adventures in Wonderland, *you'll be grinning, too, when you discover the Cheshire Crab, located on beautiful Bodkin Creek at the Pleasure Cove Marina. First you'll enjoy sampling the area's largest selection of microbrewed draft beer on a 300-seat waterfront deck. Next I suggest you try the raw bar, offering fresh bay oysters or cherrystone clams on the half shell or a hickory-smoked fish platter. The menu also lists a dozen hot appetizers and traditional American soups prepared in classic Maryland style. So follow me . . .*

WHITESTONE DILL DIP

🦀 *The last time I prepared this delicious dip, I substituted Vidalia onions for the shallots and Worcestershire sauce for the red pepper sauce. And instead of fresh vegetables, I used chips and assorted crackers. Guess what? My guest scraped the dish clean and was looking for more.*

8   ounces cream cheese, softened
1   cup mayonnaise
¼   cup dairy sour cream
½   cup snipped fresh dill
3   shallots, minced
1   beef bouillon cube, crushed
1   teaspoon red pepper sauce
8   ounces crabmeat
    assorted fresh vegetables

Beat cream cheese in medium-size bowl until light. Beat in mayonnaise and sour cream. Stir in dill, shallots, bouillon cube, red pepper sauce, and crabmeat. Refrigerate covered for several hours to blend flavors. Serve with assorted fresh vegetables.

I spotted this crab doorway in Annapolis, Maryland, at the Harbor House Restaurant around 1980. The restaurant is long gone, but my memories of the excellent crab dishes that were served here will last forever.

SCALLOPED POTATOES ROYAL OAK

Yukon Gold potatoes are perhaps the best known of the European-style yellow potatoes. They're unsurpassed in flavor and culinary versatility and actually sweeten when baked with crabmeat. Their buttery yellow flesh is excellent in this dish.

- 6 **tablespoons butter**
- 1 **onion, thinly sliced**
- 2 **tablespoons all-purpose flour**
- 2 **cups milk**
- ¾ **teaspoon salt**
- ½ **teaspoon pepper**
- 1 **cup grated Gruyère cheese**
- 3 **medium Yukon Gold potatoes, peeled and thinly sliced**
- 1 **pound crabmeat**
- ¼ **cup fresh breadcrumbs**

In a small skillet, melt 2 tablespoons butter over medium-high heat. Add onion and cook, stirring often, until translucent, about 3 minutes.

In a medium saucepan, melt remaining butter over medium heat. Add flour and cook, stirring constantly, until blended, about 2 minutes. Gradually whisk in milk, raise heat to high, and bring to a boil, whisking until thick and smooth. Reduce heat to low and simmer, whisking often, for 3 minutes. Remove from heat, season with salt and pepper, and stir in Gruyère cheese.

Spread one-third of the cheese sauce over the bottom of a lightly buttered 1½-quart casserole. Arrange half the potatoes and onions over the cheese sauce. Layer crabmeat on top with another third of the sauce. Cover with remaining potatoes and onions and the final third of the sauce. Sprinkle breadcrumbs over the top and bake uncovered for 45 minutes to 1 hour at 400°F, until potatoes are tender and top is golden brown.

Serves 4.

It's time to pick!

St. Inigoes Artichoke with Crabmeat

🦀 *The globe artichoke is cultivated mainly in California's mild coastal region. I'll never forget my visit to Castroville, California, the artichoke capital of the world. It began a love affair that's lasted more than 30 years, and I don't think it will ever end. I enjoy this recipe because it means I can eat the tasty leaves before I get to the bottoms, and then it only gets better.*

4   shallots, chopped
2   bay leaves
1   teaspoon chopped fresh thyme
      small pinch of cayenne pepper
1   teaspoon salt
4   tablespoons butter
1   pound lump crabmeat
½   cup white wine
1   egg, beaten
1   tablespoon chopped fresh parsley
½   cup breadcrumbs
6   artichoke bottoms
      Seafood Hollandaise (recipe follows)

Sauté shallots, bay leaves, thyme, cayenne and salt in the butter. Remove bay leaves. Add crabmeat , wine, egg, parsley and breadcrumbs. Make a mound of this stuffing on each artichoke bottom. Bake at 350°F for 15 minutes. Top with Seafood Hollandaise and serve.

Serves 6

SEAFOOD HOLLANDAISE:
2   extra-large eggs, beaten
5   tablespoons heavy cream
2   teaspoons lemon juice
2   teaspoons white wine vinegar
⅛   teaspoon salt
      pinch of sugar
1   teaspoon seafood seasoning
3   tablespoons unsalted butter, cut into 12
      pieces

Combine all ingredients except the butter in the top of a double boiler. Place over hot, not boiling, water that does not touch the bottom of the pan. Whisk the ingredients together well. Cook, stirring constantly, until the sauce is thick, about 5 minutes.

Whisk in the butter, 2 or 3 bits at a time, until all the butter is emulsified, 2 or 3 minutes.

I spotted this crab at the P.G.N. Crabhouse in Ocean City, Maryland. Even though I usually don't get into crab feast, this one was exceptional. People go nuts on Pete, George, and Nick's crabs. it was a pretty good night.

BELLE HAVEN CRAB SANDWICHES

Muenster cheese, or Munster cheese, as it is also known, dates back to the Middle Ages. It has been made in France and Germany, and now is made in the United States. The texture is semisoft, and the flavor ranges from mild when the cheese is young to tangy when it is aged. Regardless of where your cheese is from or the spelling, I know you're going to like these open-face sandwiches.

1   **pound crabmeat**
2   **cups packed shredded Muenster cheese**
8   **tablespoons chopped green onions**
4   **tablespoons mayonnaise**
1   **teaspoon Worcestershire sauce**
    black pepper
4   **English muffins, split**

Combine crabmeat, 1 cup cheese, 6 tablespoons green onions, mayonnaise and Worcestershire sauce in a bowl and blend. Season with black pepper to taste.

Preheat broiler. Arrange English muffin halves, split side up, on a baking sheet. Broil just until beginning to color, about 1 minute. Then mound crabmeat mixture on each muffin half. Top with remaining cheese and green onions. Broil until filling is heated through and cheese is melted. Serve hot.

Serves 4.

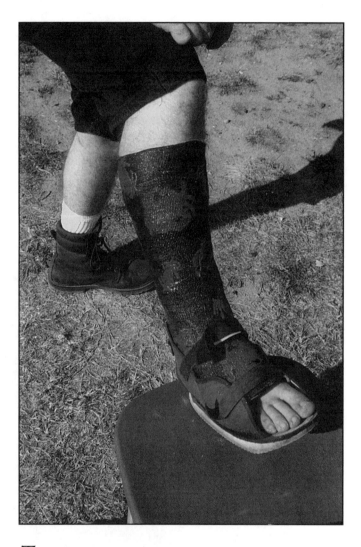

There are many festivals around the Chesapeake Bay, and the sights are numerous. When I saw Joe Keidel at the Maryland Seafood Festival with a broken leg and a crab cast, I had to get his picture. Artwork by Amy Huber.

149

SHORE BIRD STUFFED WITH CRAB

🦀 *In about an hour, this shore bird stuffed with crab can be ready for guests. Usually half a hen is an ample serving for one person, but when it's stuffed with crabmeat, and when several side dishes are offered, you can serve six friends easily. Try it with wild rice and fresh carrots!*

8   slices bacon, chopped in ½-inch pieces
6   shallots, chopped
1   stick butter
3   cups 2-day-old bread, cubed
8   ounces crabmeat
½   cup chopped fresh parsley
2   tablespoons dry white wine
2   eggs, lightly beaten
    salt and pepper

seafood seasoning
1   roasting hen, approximately 3 pounds

In a skillet, sauté the bacon until crisp. Drain on paper towels and reserve. In another skillet, sauté shallots in butter until soft. Remove with a slotted spoon and reserve. Sauté bread cubes in the butter remaining in the pan until golden. In a bowl, combine the bread cubes, bacon, shallots, crabmeat, parsley, wine, eggs and salt, pepper and seafood seasoning to taste.

Pack hen loosely with this stuffing and roast at 375°F until juices run clear or an instant thermometer registers 170°F, about 1 hour, 15 minutes.

Serves 6.

Photograph by Vince Lupo

*P*icking hard crab is an art requiring both dexterity and a certain etiquette. Anybody can smash a crab with a knife handle or a wooden mallet. But professional crab pickers and those who prize large chunks of sweet meat, free of shells, use only a small, sharp knife with a heavy handle. I favor the "crab knife" manufactured by Carvel Hall in Crisfield, Maryland. This picture is art!

150

BACK CREEK CRAB CAKES WITH BASIL

🦀 *These crab cakes are extraordinarily tasty because of the addition of Basil Sauce, roasted red pepper and grated lemon peel. The result is a refreshing new kind of crab cake. You may broil the cakes rather than fry them, but they will not be quite as moist or have the lovely texture that frying produces.*

CRAB CAKES:
- 1 pound crabmeat
- 1 roasted red pepper, minced
  Basil Sauce (recipe follows)
- 1½ teaspoons grated lemon peel
- 2 cups fresh breadcrumbs (from about 8 ounces of French bread)
- 2 large egg yolks
  all-purpose flour for dredging
- 2 egg whites, beaten just until foamy
- 3 tablespoons butter

Combine crabmeat, red pepper, 3 tablespoons Basil Sauce and lemon peel in a large bowl. Mix in 1 cup breadcrumbs and season to taste with salt and pepper. Mix in egg yolks (mixture will be soft).

Form crab mixture into eight cakes. Coat cakes on both sides with flour; shake off excess. Brush both sides of cakes with beaten egg whites, then coat with remaining breadcrumbs. Cover and chill for 4 hours.

Melt butter in a large skillet over medium-high heat. Working in batches, cook cakes until golden brown and heated through, about 4 minutes on each side. Place two cakes on each plate and serve with remaining Basil Sauce.

Serves 4.

BASIL SAUCE:
- ¾ cup mayonnaise
- ⅓ cup finely chopped fresh basil
- 1 tablespoon fresh lemon juice
- 2 teaspoons minced garlic
- 1½ teaspoons grated lemon peel
  salt and pepper

Mix mayonnaise, basil, lemon juice, garlic and lemon peel in a medium bowl. Season to taste with salt and pepper. Cover and refrigerate at least one hour to allow flavors to develop.

Crisfield quotation: "When the crabs are running, the money is running."

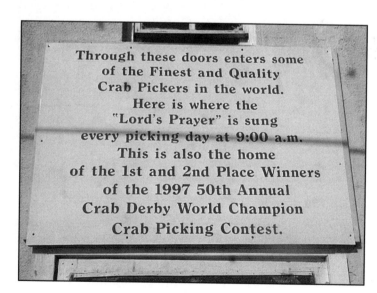

Through these doors enters some of the Finest and Quality Crab Pickers in the world. Here is where the "Lord's Prayer" is sung every picking day at 9:00 a.m. This is also the home of the 1st and 2nd Place Winners of the 1997 50th Annual Crab Derby World Champion Crab Picking Contest.

CRAB SHACK SWEET CORN SOUP

Although there are fewer variations of cream of crab soup than there are of the Maryland crab soup (vegetable style), Chesapeake chefs rely on tradition and ingenuity to guide them through a complete soup repertoire. In this soup it's the sweet cream-style corn that enhances the taste of the succulent crab.

3½ **cups chicken stock**
12 **ounces cream-style corn**
8 **ounces crabmeat**
  salt and pepper
1 **teaspoon light soy sauce**
2 **tablespoons cornstarch**
3 **tablespoons stock**
2 **egg whites**
4 **green onions, sliced diagonally**
2 **hard-boiled egg yolks**

Bring the stock to a boil in a large pan. Add the corn, crabmeat, salt and pepper to taste and soy sauce, and simmer for 5 minutes.

Mix the cornstarch and 3 tablespoons stock and then add a spoonful of the hot soup. Add this mixture back to the soup and bring back to a boil. Cook until the soup thickens.

Just before serving, beat the egg whites until soft peaks form and stir into the hot soup . Garnish with green onion slices and hard-boiled egg yolks passed through a sieve.

Serves 4.

Shedding boxes, Deal Island, circa 1997.

CRAB-STUFFED SHRIMP

This recipe works best with the largest shrimp you can find. I like to use those that weight out at 12 to a pound—that way you can serve them as an appetizer or a main dish.

6	cups water
1	small onion, halved
1	lemon, quartered
1	rib celery, quartered
2	cloves garlic, halved
12	peppercorns
1	sprig fresh parsley
1	pound shrimp
8	ounces crabmeat
2	tablespoons mayonnaise
1	tablespoon sour cream
1	tablespoon lemon juice
1	teaspoon minced fresh tarragon
½	teaspoon grated lemon peel
	minced fresh parsley

In a large saucepan, heat the water, onion, lemon, celery, garlic, peppercorns and parsley sprig to boiling; boil for 5 minutes. Add shrimp; bring to a boil again and boil until shrimp are completely opaque, about 5 minutes. Remove shrimp from broth with a slotted spoon and refrigerate until cold.

Shell and devein shrimp, leaving tails intact. Split them lengthwise three-quarters of the way through the back. Combine crabmeat, mayonnaise, sour cream, lemon juice, tarragon and lemon peel in a small bowl. Stuff crabmeat mixture into shrimp. Dip stuffed edge into minced parsley. Refrigerate, covered, for 1 hour.

Serves 6.

My memory has failed me once again. I know I stopped and scraped the dirt from my shoes. I know I feasted on crab and beer. But I don't know where I was when I took this picture!

CORN, CRAB AND CHEDDAR CHOWDER

🦀 *The name "chowder" commemorates the pot in which this dish was once cooked. The soup seems to have originated in Newfoundland, where any fish that came to hand went into it. In Chesapeake Country, corn and crab are readily available. The addition of Cheddar cheese is a natural and lends itself well to this fabulous concoction.*

1 **tablespoon unsalted butter**
1 **onion, chopped**
¾ **pound red-skinned potatoes, peeled and diced**
2 **cups corn kernels**
2 **cups half and half**
2 **cup (or more) canned vegetable broth**

1 **tablespoon chopped fresh thyme**
8 **ounces crabmeat**
2 **cups grated medium-sharp cheddar cheese (about 6 ounces)**
   salt and pepper

Melt butter in a heavy medium-size saucepan over medium-high heat. Add onion; sauté until tender, about 5 minutes. Add potatoes, corn, half-and-half, broth and thyme. Cover pan partially and simmer until potatoes are tender, about 15 minutes. Add crabmeat and cheese; stir until cheese is melted. Season with salt and pepper.

Serves 4.

A visit to Chick's Oyster Bar in Virginia Beach, Virginia, has many rewards. It's fun from the moment you arrive—just look for this feisty crab painted on the side of the building, and then look for the Baltimore Crabfeast. You start with a pitcher of beer and two bowls of chowder and follow that with a half dozen steamed crabs and two crab cake sandwiches. And there's more! Stop by and see what I mean. Just look for the crab.

154

MARSH POINT STUFFED CLAMSHELLS

🦀 *Stuffing clam and oyster shells is as old as the Bay itself. There are countless ways to use the shells. Seafood lovers will appreciate the variety that this dish offers. The sweet pickle relish, the crunch of the cucumbers and the bite of the onions and garlic all add to the sophistication of the dish.*

1 **pound crabmeat**
2 **tablespoons peeled, diced and drained cucumber**
2 **tablespoons sweet pickle relish, drained**
2 **tablespoons cocktail sauce**
1 **tablespoon finely chopped onion**
1 **tablespoon finely chopped garlic**

salt
1 **hard-boiled egg worked through a ricer**
mayonnaise
36 **clamshells, washed and dried**
minced fresh parsley

Combined crabmeat, cucumber, pickle relish, cocktail sauce, onion, garlic, and salt to taste. Stir in enough mayonnaise to bind the mixture and fold in hard-boiled egg. Put a generous tablespoon of the mixture into each clamshell, sprinkle the tops with parsley, and chill until serving time.

Serves 6 to 8.

*Chesapeake Bay clams come in many sizes and shapes, and with many spellings, but I like to keep it simple like most Chesapeake chefs do. They refer to them as either soft-shell clams (*manninose *or* manoes*) or hard-shell clams. Hard-shell clams include cherrystones, surf clams and littlenecks. All are great steamed, raw on the half-shell, fried, and in chowders and stews. The next time you prepare clam chowder, save the shells and stuff them with crabmeat.*

STEAMED CRABS
MANOES
CRABS TO GO

SMALL BOAT HARBOR PIZZA WITH CRAB

There was a time when it was thought that pizza could be found only in Italy. As we well know, pizza can now be found in practically every country of the world, and it need not be just a snack or a quick-cooked meal—it can become an elegant main dish, as in this recipe. The preparation is simple. The three cheeses complement the luscious crabmeat.

1   uncooked 14-inch pizza crust
1   can (28 ounces) whole tomatoes, individually squeezed and left to drain
8   ounces crabmeat
2   green onions, sliced
¼   cup sliced yellow pepper
2   ounces mozzarella cheese, grated

2   ounces mild provolone cheese, grated
3   ounces sharp white cheddar cheese, grated

Spread tomatoes on pizza dough to within a half inch of edge. Top with crabmeat, onion, pepper, mozzarella, provolone and then cheddar cheeses. Bake 10 to 15 minutes at 400°F until golden brown.

Serves 2 to 4.

Getting out on the Bay is sometimes a challenge for those of us unwilling to accept the responsibility of owning a boat. That's why I enjoy the many small boat harbors and the thousands of nooks and crannies surrounded by waterways and laced with creeks and inlets. The Chesapeake is filled with breathtaking natural beauty.

REMINGTON FARMS PINEAPPLE-CRAB SALAD

Remington Farms, near Chestertown, Maryland, is a great place to observe tens of thousands of Canada geese, mallards, pintails, and other types of ducks during seasonal migrations. You can explore the 3000-acre wildlife area using a free brochure with a self-guided driving tour. My suggestion is to prepare this delightful crab and pineapple salad, pack the cooler, load up the kids and head on out. Enjoy!

4   ripe pineapples
2   pounds crabmeat
   Bayside Dressing (recipe follows)

Halve the pineapples lengthwise. Cut out the pulp, leaving a shell about ½-inch thick, and chill the shells. Remove the core from the pulp and dice the pulp. In a bowl, combine the diced pineapple with the crabmeat.

Combine dressing with the pineapple and crabmeat mixture and spoon the salad into the chilled pineapple shells.

Serves 8.

BAYSIDE DRESSING:
1   cup mayonnaise
⅔   cup ketchup
1   tablespoon lemon juice
1   tablespoon Worcestershire sauce
1   tablespoon brandy
3   drops Tabasco sauce
   mint sprigs

Mix all ingredients in a bowl.

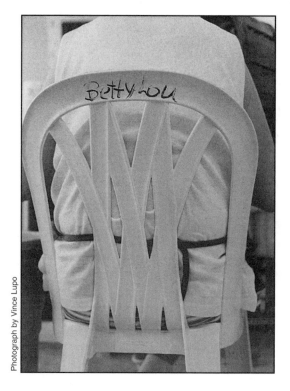

Photograph by Vince Lupo

T hat's Betty Lou's chair, so park yourself someplace else. Smith Island Ladies' Co-op, circa 1998.

UPPER FERRY CRAB SANDWICHES

Monterey Jack cheese was so named because it originated in Monterey, California. It is buttery-ivory in color, semisoft in texture, and has a mild, somewhat bland flavor. It has high moisture and good melting properties, making it excellent for these crab sandwiches.

8	ounces crabmeat
¼	cup finely chopped celery
¼	cup finely chopped sweet pickle
1	hard-boiled egg, finely chopped
1	scallion, finely chopped
¼	cup mayonnaise
1	large tomato cut into 4 slices
4	English muffins, split and toasted
4	slices Monterey Jack cheese
	paprika
	chopped fresh parsley

Mix together the crabmeat, celery, pickles, egg, scallion, and mayonnaise. Place 1 tomato slice on each of 4 muffin halves. Top with crabmeat mixture and a slice of cheese. Sprinkle with paprika and broil 5 inches from the source of heat until the cheese melts. Garnish with parsley. Serve with remaining muffin halves.

Serves 4.

Tennis anyone? Racquetball? Horseshoes?

Skipjack Races Crab Sandwiches

🦀 *Skipjack races are held on Labor Day weekend on tiny Deal Island on Maryland's Eastern Shore. The accompanying festival includes a fishing tournament, crab pot pulling contest, boat docking and much, much more.*

8	**ounces crabmeat**
2	**hard-boiled eggs, minced**
1	**tablespoon minced fresh dill**
¼	**cup minced dill pickle**
¼	**cup mayonnaise**
1	**tablespoon lemon juice**
½	**teaspoon salt**
½	**teaspoon black pepper**
¼	**teaspoon cayenne pepper**
6	**slices white bread, crust trimmed** **butter**
6	**slices peeled tomato**
6	**tablespoons grated Parmigiano-** **Reggiano cheese**

Combine crabmeat, eggs, dill, dill pickle, mayonnaise, lemon juice, salt, black pepper and cayenne pepper; mix well. Toast bread and butter lightly. Top each slice of bread with crab mixture, a slice of tomato, and a tablespoon of Parmesan cheese. Place on a baking sheet and bake at 400°F until the cheese has melted.

Serves 3.

*N*o, this is not a skipjack but a crab scraper, a boat designed and built by Buster Nelson, Crisfield, Maryland. The boat is used for dragging a crab scrape (rake) through the grass to strain out peelers and soft-shell crabs.

KITTY KNIGHT CRAB OMELET

🦀 *One of the best things about omelets is their unique adaptability. You can start with a basic omelet recipe and enhance it with a pinch of herbs, a creamy sauce, or toasted pine nuts.*

FILLING:

8	ounces crabmeat
2	teaspoons lemon juice
¼	cup toasted slivered almonds plus additional for serving
3	tablespoons finely chopped onion
¼	teaspoon dried dill weed
	dash of white pepper
1	tablespoon butter

OMELET:

5	eggs
2	tablespoons water
1	teaspoon salt
⅛	teaspoon black pepper
2	tablespoons butter
2	tablespoons dairy sour cream plus additional for serving
	fresh dill

Filling: Combine crabmeat with lemon juice in a small bowl; stir in ¼ cup almonds, onion, dill, and white pepper. Cook and stir mixture in 1 tablespoon butter in a skillet over low heat until hot, about 2 minutes. Keep warm.

Omelet: Beat eggs, water, salt, black pepper and 2 tablespoons sour cream until just blended. Heat a 10-inch omelet pan with sloping sides over low heat for 1 minute; add 2 tablespoons butter. Tilt pan to coat bottom and sides with melted butter. When foam subsides, add egg mixture. Cook over low heat, without stirring, until lightly browned on underside, about 10 minutes.

Spoon filling down center of omelet; fold opposite sides of omelet over filling to form a roll. Top with a dollop of sour cream and garnish with toasted almonds and fresh dill. Serve immediately.

Serves 2 to 4.

Lazy Susans Policy: No ID . . . No Service!!!. Whitey's Policy: No cook crabs to order, no eat there!

SHARP STREET WHARF CRAB SALAD

🦀 *Crabmeat salad, a refreshing and welcome complement to a summer menu, may be composed of a medley of ingredients, all of which can be selected with an eye on one's purse as well as an eye on a palate attuned to excellent flavor.*

- 8 ounces crabmeat
- 2 dill pickles, finely chopped
- 1 tablespoon capers, drained, and chopped
  zest of 1 lime, finely grated
- 2 tablespoons fresh lime juice
- 1 shallot, finely chopped
- 1 tablespoon white wine
- 1 tablespoon olive oil
- 3 drops Tabasco sauce
  salt and freshly ground black pepper
- 3 cups salad greens
  sweet pickles

Combine all ingredients except salad greens and sweet pickles in a bowl, then divide the mixture in half. Pile each half on a plate and form it into a round, flattened shape about 1/2-inch high. Garnish with salad greens and sweet pickles.
Serves 2.

I spotted this truck on Solomons Island. It passed by so quickly, I didn't have time to take a photograph. When I came across the same vehicle parked, I knew I had to get a picture.

RAINBOW TROUT WITH CRAB SAUCE

🦀 *Probably the best-known of the fresh water trout, the rainbow is now readily available, thanks to fish hatcheries. Rainbows can grow up to 5 pounds, but most commercially raised fish average about 8 ounces.*

4   **rainbow trout (6 ounces each)**
    salt and pepper
3   **eggs, beaten into 1 tablespoon ice water**
1   **cup all-purpose flour**
6   **tablespoons clarified butter**
4   **tablespoons butter**
½   **cup minced shallots**
2   **tablespoons capers, drained**
8   **ounces crabmeat**
1   **tablespoon minced fresh parsley**
1   **clove garlic, minced**
    juice of 1 lemon
    lemon halves
    cherry tomatoes
    parsley sprigs

Clean the trout, leaving the heads and tails intact. Rinse, pat dry, and sprinkle with salt and pepper. Dip in the beaten egg, dredge in the flour, shaking off the excess, and in a skillet, sauté them in the clarified butter over moderate heat for 4 minutes on each side, or until they flake easily when tested with a fork. Transfer trout to a heated platter and keep warm.

Wipe out the skillet, add 4 tablespoons butter, and in it sauté shallots and capers until shallots are soft. Add crabmeat, minced parsley and garlic and sauté for 1 minute. Add lemon juice and spoon the mixture over the trout.

Garnish with lemon halves, cherry tomatoes and parsley sprigs.

Serves 4.

Crabs, $6.00 a dozen. I took this picture in Linkwood, Maryland, in 1984. In 1999, in Bethany Beach, Delaware, I paid $60 for a dozen crabs!

CATCH OF THE DAY ON ICE

🦀 *An impressive seafood display can be so lavish that you need nothing else on your hors d'oeuvres table, or it can be cut down in size and presented along with other dishes.*

- 1   **dozen oysters, shucked and on half shell**
- 1   **pound shrimp, cooked and peeled with tail intact**
- 1   **pound jumbo lump crabmeat**
- 1   **dozen clams, shucked and on half shell**
     Seafood-Cocktail Sauce (recipe follows)

Arrange seafood selection on crushed ice on a large platter.

SEAFOOD-COCKTAIL SAUCE
- ½   **cup chili sauce**
- 1   **tablespoon prepared horseradish**
- 1   **tablespoon lemon juice**
- 2   **teaspoons Worcestershire sauce**
- ¼   **teaspoon salt**
     dash of cayenne pepper

In a small bowl, combine all ingredients; mix well and refrigerate, covered, at least 3 hours before serving.

Makes ⅔ cup.

*A**re you hungry yet?***

163

ISLAND GIRL CRAB AND PINEAPPLE SALAD

🦀 *During the hot Chesapeake summers, you will find me out back on the screened porch, usually picking a crab or two. Sometimes a crab salad is what I have in mind, so I only eat the claw meat and save what's left for my salad. Sometimes the salad can be as simple as serving the best chunks of crabmeat over crisp lettuce with lemon juice and capers, and sometimes it can be a little more complicated, like this recipe. If you decide to make this one, keep in mind that pineapples can sometimes be a little tart. If that's the case, add a pinch of sugar to the dressing.*

1   **pound crabmeat**
1   **cup cooked rice, cooled**
1   **cup ½-inch pineapple pieces**
2   **red delicious apples, peeled and diced**
3   **tablespoons snipped fresh dill**
    iceberg lettuce
    buttercrunch lettuce
    romaine lettuce
    dill sprigs
    Smithmap Dressing (recipe follows)

In a bowl, combine crabmeat, rice, pineapple, apples and dill. Line salad bowls with lettuce leaves and mound crabmeat mixture on top. Pour the dressing over the crabmeat, garnish with sprigs of dill, and toss just before serving.

Serves 6.

SMITHMAP DRESSING:
  ¾   **cup mayonnaise**
  2   **tablespoons pineapple juice**
  1   **tablespoon lemon juice**
  ¼   **teaspoon seafood seasoning**
  ½   **teaspoon paprika**
    salt to taste

Mix all ingredients.

Bushel baskets are being phased out around the Chesapeake. Baskets are being replaced by cardboard boxes with a red crab stamped on the side. Sure they hold a bushel of crabs, but for me it's not the same; the bushel basket has nobility.

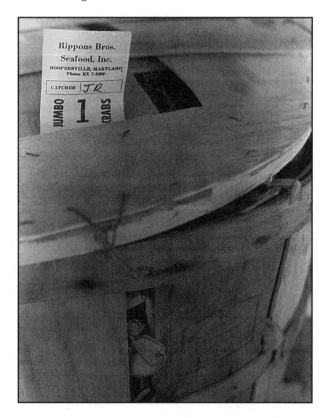

CHAPTER 8
Crabbers

Photograph by Melissa G. Dole, Maryland Watermen's Association

PAULINE'S SOFT-SHELL CRABS

🦀 *The actual shedding of a crab's shell, when it finally cracks open and the soft crab backs out, takes anywhere from one to three hours. If the crab is not removed from the water immediately, the hardening process will commence, causing a reduction in the quality of the soft-shell crab. Crabs that have been left in the water too long form a shell that feels leathery. These crabs are called "paper shells" or "buckrams."*

- 12 **soft-shell crabs**
- 1 **cup all-purpose flour**
- 1 **teaspoon salt**
- 1 **teaspoon pepper**
- 3 **tablespoons butter**
- 3 **tablespoons olive oil**
- 3 **tablespoons fresh lime juice**
- ½ **cup chopped fresh cilantro**

Dry crabs thoroughly on paper towels. Place flour in a shallow bowl. Dredge crabs lightly in the flour, place them on a large platter, and season with salt and pepper.

In a large skillet, melt butter in oil over high heat. Add crabs and cook, turning once, until lightly browned, 3 minutes per side, in two batches if necessary. Use additional butter and oil if needed.

Squeeze lime juice over the cooked crabs and garnish with chopped cilantro. Serve hot.

Serves 4.

*B*uster Nelson: *"We've dredged up some strange things. I've pulled in an axe head that dates 5,000 years ago, but I've heard stories of a waterman pulling in a lady's pocketbook with ninety-seven dollars in it. Now that's a good catch."*

SAXIS BROILED SOFT-SHELL CRABS

🦀 *Prior to the actual molting process, a crab will begin to show signs that tell the experienced crabber how soon it will be until the crab will shed. As the time for molting approaches, the new shell of the crab will begin to form and become visible as a line underneath the old hard shell. The point where it becomes most visible is along the edges of the flattened sections of the paddle fins.*

6	tablespoons butter
2	tablespoons olive oil
1	medium onion, minced
3	cloves garlic, minced
3	Roma tomatoes, peeled, seeded and chopped
2	cups cooked navy beans
1	teaspoon salt
1	teaspoon pepper
1-3	tablespoons fresh lime juice
12	soft-shell crabs
2	tablespoons chopped fresh parsley

In a large skillet, melt 2 tablespoons of the butter with the olive oil over medium heat. Add onion and garlic and cook, stirring occasionally, until translucent, about 3 minutes. Raise heat to medium-high, add tomatoes, and cook, stirring, until thick and pulpy, about 5 minutes. Stir in navy beans, salt, and pepper and cook until beans are warmed through. Remove from heat and cover to keep warm.

In a small saucepan, melt remaining butter over low heat. Remove from heat and stir in lime juice. Place crabs on their backs on a broiling pan and brush lightly with some of the butter mixture.

Broil crabs 4 inches from heat until lightly browned, about 3 minutes. Turn, brush with remaining butter mixture, and broil until lightly browned, about 3 minutes longer. To serve, place tomato/navy bean mixture on plates and top with two crabs each. Garnish with chopped parsley.

Serves 6.

In early stages of molting, the line of the new shell is white, which indicates that the crab will molt within 2 weeks. Gradually, as molting time nears, the line goes through a series of color changes: a pink line means molting within a week, a red line indicates a molting within one to three days. These red sign crabs are also known as "peelers," since they're getting ready to "peel off" their shells.

Buster Nelson skillfully checks his floats.

167

BROILED SOFT-SHELL CRABS WITH GARLIC BUTTER

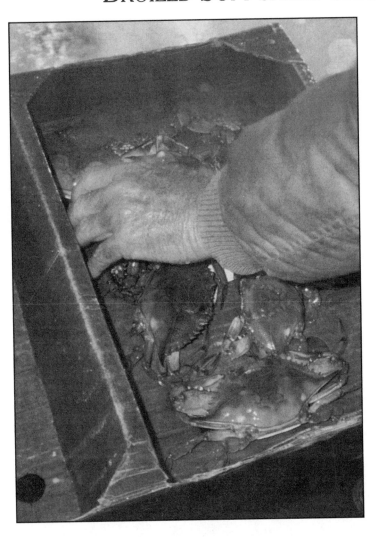

🦀 *The moment a friend read this recipe, his first response was "Why orange marmalade?" Why? Because when you try as many soft-shell crab recipes as I do, you need a change once in a while. In one week at the crab lab (my kitchen), we had soft crabs with the following sauces: Coconut Curry Sauce, Black Bean Sauce, Balsamic Vinegar & Raspberry Sauce, and Peach Papaya Salsa. As you can see, the possibilities are endless!*

12   soft-shell crabs
½   teaspoon salt
¼   teaspoon pepper
1   stick butter, melted
1   tablespoon fresh lemon juice
4   garlic cloves, minced
1   tablespoon chopped fresh parsley
     orange marmalade

Preheat broiler. Place crabs on their backs on a broiling pan and season with salt and pepper. In a small bowl, combine butter, lemon juice, garlic and parsley. Stir well to blend. Brush crabs liberally with this garlic butter. Broil about 4 inches from heat until golden brown on top, about 4 minutes. Turn crabs over, brush with remaining garlic butter, and continue broiling until nicely browned and cooked through, about 3 minutes longer. Garnish with orange marmalade and serve with cole slaw.

Serves 4.

*A*lmost all commercial production of soft-shell crabs comes from shedding operations in which hard crabs are held either in floating pens or in tables onshore until they shed their hard shells. The moment they become soft-shell crabs, they are removed from the flats and made ready for market.

BROILED SOFT CRABS WITH RED PEPPER SAUCE

🦀 *Stuffing soft-shell crabs with a crabmeat mixture makes a dramatic presentation. It's a perfect dish for crab lovers who feel that soft-shells do not have enough meat in them.*

1   tablespoon fresh breadcrumbs
1   tablespoon mayonnaise
½   teaspoon lemon juice
3   shakes Tabasco sauce
⅓   teaspoon Worcestershire sauce
⅓   cup crabmeat
    salt and freshly ground black pepper
4   soft-shell crabs
    Red Pepper Sauce (recipe follows)

Combine breadcrumbs, mayonnaise, lemon juice, Tabasco sauce, Worcestershire sauce, crabmeat and salt and pepper. Under the top shell of each soft-shell crab, on both ends, stuff one to two teaspoons of this mixture where the gills were. Fold the shell back over. Broil crabs until golden brown, turning often until they are crisp on the outside and hot on the inside. To serve, center each crab on a plate and spoon Red Pepper Sauce over and around it.

Serves 4.

RED PEPPER SAUCE
1   large red bell pepper
½   cup olive oil
2   tablespoons red wine vinegar
1   clove garlic, minced
1   shallot, minced
¼   teaspoon salt

Place the pepper on a baking sheet and bake for 25 minutes at 350°F, turning every 5 minutes until the skin is blackened. Remove the pepper from the oven and put it immediately into a paper bag and close it tightly. When the pepper is cool enough to touch, remove it from the bag and peel off the skin. Discard the stem and seeds. Cut the pepper into large chunks and place them into a blender. Add 2 tablespoons of the oil and puree until smooth. Add the remaining oil, vinegar, garlic, shallot, and salt; process until well blended. Set aside.

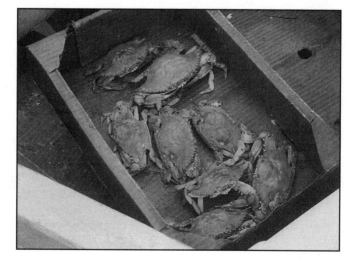

*T*he soft crab fishery is a seasonal one. As water temperatures drop, the activity, and hence molting, of blue crabs begins to slow. Water temperatures over 70°F are best for active shedding. In the Chesapeake, soft-shell crabs are produced from the late spring to early fall, with May through August the most productive months.

169

RED SHANTY STUFFED MUSHROOMS

This hearty combination of mushrooms and crab with ripe brie cheese is a perfect complement to any party. If the mushrooms are large, you can make this as an entrée, but I like to use mushrooms that are no larger than a fifty-cent piece.

2	tablespoons olive oil
2	pounds mushrooms
1	teaspoon salt
½	teaspoon black pepper
1	pound crabmeat
½	pound brie cheese
½	cup chopped fresh parsley

Brush a large baking dish with olive oil. Remove stems from mushrooms and reserve for another use. Wipe caps clean with a damp cloth. Season cavities with salt, pepper and a pinch of parsley. Cut brie into ½-inch pieces. Fill each mushroom cap with crabmeat and top with a piece of brie. Place in the oiled baking dish.

Bake at 375°F until cheese is bubbly and lightly browned, about 10 minutes. Garnish with chopped parsley and serve hot.

Serves 20 to 30 as an appetizer.

Young crabs hatched in the mouth of the Bay soon begin moving up the Bay and into the tributaries. When they reach Maryland waters, they are usually about one to one-and-a-half inches across the carapace (back). When these appear in large numbers in the spring in Tangier Sound, the crabbers know they are going to have a good season. These small crabs feed, grow rapidly and molt frequently, increasing about one-third in size with each molt.

CRAB-STUFFED ZUCCHINI BOWLERS WHARF

🦀 *The off-white flesh of a zucchini has a very pale green cast, and the flavor is light and delicate. For this reason, zucchini is the perfect vegetable to highlight sweet, succulent crabmeat. When it comes to selecting zucchini for this dish, try to use only those 8 inches long—anything else will be less appealing.*

4   **8-inch zucchini, cut in half lengthwise**
1   **teaspoon salt**
1   **teaspoon pepper**
1   **pound crabmeat**
½   **cup dried breadcrumbs**
½   **cup grated Parmigiano-Reggiano cheese**
4   **tablespoons melted butter**

Use a small spoon to scrape out pulp from zucchini halves, leaving a shell about ¼-inch thick. Discard pulp. Season shells with ½ teaspoon each salt and pepper. Fill zucchini halves with crabmeat and season with remaining salt and pepper.

In a small bowl, combine breadcrumbs and Parmigiano-Reggiano cheese. Sprinkle about 1 tablespoon over each zucchini half. Drizzle with melted butter. Place in an oiled baking dish and bake at 400°F until lightly browned, about 20 minutes. Serve immediately.

Serves 8.

*W*atermen start crabbing in April, but they spend the winter getting ready—crab pots are in constant need of repair. Pictured here is Brick Thompson, who enjoys a comfortable seat, a sunny day, and a nice location along the Potomac River in Colonial Beach, Virginia, while he mends crab pots.

171

Solomons Harbor Crab Au Gratin

A gratin is any dish that is topped with cheese or breadcrumbs and bits of butter and then heated in the oven or under the broiler until golden brown and crispy. I choose not to add butter to the topping, but if you want to add it, feel free to do so.

3	**tablespoons butter**
3	**tablespoons all-purpose flour**
3½	**cups milk**
1	**cup grated Swiss cheese**
1	**teaspoon salt**
1	**teaspoon pepper**
1	**pound crabmeat**
½	**cup dry breadcrumbs**
½	**cup grated Parmigiano-Reggiano cheese**

Melt butter in a saucepan over medium heat. Add flour and cook, stirring often, without allowing flour to color. Whisk milk in gradually. Bring to a boil, whisking often, until sauce is creamy and smooth, about 5 minutes. Reduce heat and simmer 3 minutes longer. Remove from heat, stir in Swiss cheese, and season with salt and pepper. Set aside to cool slightly.

Preheat oven to 425°F. Stir crabmeat into cheese sauce and transfer to a buttered baking dish. Sprinkle breadcrumbs and Parmigiano-Reggiano cheese over the top. Bake until golden brown, about 15 minutes.

Serves 6.

Near the mouth of the Patuxent River, Solomons Island beckons to boaters cruising the Bay. The harbor is well protected and the creeks fanning from it provide endless opportunities for crabbers. It's here that I photographed this workboat.

BACK CREEK CRAB MASH

For me, potatoes are much more than a mere accompaniment—they're a vital ingredient and an invaluable cooking aid. In this dish, the mashed potatoes cradle the crabmeat and add greatly to the overall flavor.

> **3   cups mashed potatoes, seasoned with salt and pepper**
> **1   pound lump crabmeat**
> **¾   cup Ritz cracker crumbs**
> **2   tablespoons melted butter**
>   **Medium White Sauce (recipe follows)**

Line a well-buttered baking dish with mashed potatoes and bake at 400°F until slightly browned. Fill the dish with crabmeat heated in a cup of Medium White Sauce. Sprinkle with Ritz cracker crumbs mixed with melted butter, and bake at 350°F until crumbs are browned.

Serves 6.

MEDIUM WHITE SAUCE
> **1   cup hot milk**
> **2   tablespoons butter**
> **2   tablespoons all-purpose flour**
> **¼   teaspoon salt**
> **⅛   teaspoon pepper**

Scald the milk. Melt the butter in a saucepan over low heat. Add flour, stirring constantly. Stir in the hot milk gradually and cook, stirring constantly, until the mixture thickens.

I spotted The Big Crab *while enjoying lunch on Tilghman Island. I'll let you guess what I had for lunch! Let's just say I came, I crushed, I conquered.*

THE BIG CRAB

SOFT-SHELL CRABS WITH LEMON THYME

🦀 *No herb garden worth the name should be without some thyme. There are many species, all highly aromatic and attractive. My favorite thymes to grow are golden thyme and variegated lemon thyme.*

12	soft-shell crabs
1½	cups buttermilk
1	cup all-purpose flour
2	tablespoons chopped fresh lemon thyme leaves
1	teaspoon salt
½	teaspoon black pepper
½	teaspoon cayenne pepper
2	tablespoons butter
2	tablespoons vegetable oil
	lemon wedges
	lemon thyme sprigs

In a large bowl, marinate crabs in buttermilk for 30 minutes at room temperature. In a shallow bowl, combine flour, lemon thyme, salt, black pepper and cayenne pepper. Remove crabs from the buttermilk, drain off excess, and dredge in the seasoned flour to coat both sides lightly.

In a large skillet, melt butter with oil over medium-high heat. Add crabs and cook, turning once, until lightly browned, about 3 minutes per side. Cook in 2 batches if necessary, using additional butter and oil if needed. Serve hot with lemon wedges and sprigs of lemon thyme.

Serves 4.

Photograph by Vince Lupo

*W*hat's in a name? A lot.

LOVE POINT CHEESECAKE

🦀 *The word "cheesecake" dates back to the early fifteenth century. At that time it meant a "cooked tart." In today's kitchen, we tend to think of cheesecake as a luscious, rich dessert, but we suggest you serve this dish as an appetizer. Your guests will love it.*

2   **slices fresh bread, crust removed, made into breadcrumbs**
¼   **cup grated Parmigiano-Reggiano cheese**
1   **large sweet onion, diced**
4   **cloves garlic, minced**
    butter for sautéeing
1   **pound cream cheese**
1   **pound ricotta cheese**
¼   **cup all-purpose flour**
5   **eggs**
3   **egg yolks**
⅓   **cup heavy cream**
3   **cups grated sharp cheddar cheese**

2   **large red bell peppers, roasted, seeded and chopped**
2   **large yellow bell peppers, roasted, seeded and chopped**
1   **pound lump crabmeat**

Butter a 10-inch springform pan. Combine breadcrumbs and Parmesan cheese and sprinkle over the bottom of the pan. In a skillet, sauté onion and garlic in a small amount of butter until translucent. Using an electric mixer, beat together the cream cheese, ricotta, flour, eggs, egg yolks and cream. Fold in onion/garlic mixture, Cheddar, roasted peppers, and crabmeat. Place pan in a water bath filled with 2 inches of boiling water. Bake at 250°F for 1 hour and 40 minutes. Turn off heat and leave in oven for another hour. Remove and let cool for several hours or overnight before unmolding.

Serves a crowd.

Photograph by Melissa G. Dole, Maryland Watermen's Association

*W*aterman: "We 'fish' approximately 800 crab pots that have been sitting for a couple of days. Once we empty a pot, we shovel a couple of handfuls of clams or fish into the its cylindrical bait chamber. As the crew brings a full pot into the boat, a freshly baited pot is tossed into the Bay where the full pot came out. This way the floats stay in the same area each day and in a relatively straight line."

SMOKEY POINT SEAFOOD SURPRISE

🦀 *This dish appears on many Bay Country restaurant menus, usually without the rice and soft-shell crabs. It's no surprise that it will be gracefully received by your guests. And if you've been searching for a zesty, vibrant, dry, crisp white wine that goes with almost any crab dish, look no further than Sauvignon Blanc.*

2	**cups cooked rice**
½	**pound bay scallops**
½	**pound medium shrimp, shelled and deveined**
8	**ounces crabmeat**
2	**soft-shell crabs, cut in half**
4	**tablespoons butter, melted**
¼	**cup fresh lemon juice**
¼	**teaspoon salt**
¼	**teaspoon pepper**
	seafood seasoning
1	**tablespoon chopped fresh parsley**

Cut four pieces of aluminum foil measuring 15 inches by 15 inches. In the center of each, place a half-cup of rice. Top rice with scallops, shrimp, crabmeat and half of a soft-shell crab. Drizzle 1 tablespoon butter over each mound and sprinkle with lemon juice. Season with salt, pepper and seafood seasoning. Add a pinch of parsley.

Fold foil to make packets and crimp edges to seal tightly. Arrange packets in a single layer on a baking sheet, bake at 425°F for 10 to 12 minutes, and test for doneness. Serve hot.

Serves 4.

Thousands of crab pots are set in the Bay each year. The metal traps sit on the bottom and are tied to float markers on the surface. In the spring, most crab pots are put near shore in shallow water. In summer, they can be found in mid-Bay and deeper water.

Photograph by Melissa G. Dole, Maryland Watermen's Association

STEWED JIMMIES

🦀 *This recipe is from Mary T. Evans of Salisbury, Maryland. Mary says the dish has been in her family for as long as she can remember. Jimmies are male crabs. They are the best to use for steaming, and can be distinguished from the females by an inverted "T" shape on their undershells.*

12-15 **live male crabs with back shells and loose innards (including attached gills) removed**
  1 **quart tap water**
  6 **strips bacon**
  2 **tablespoons all-purpose flour**
  2 **medium onions, diced**
     salt and pepper
6-8 **medium potatoes, peeled**
     Dumplings (recipe follows)
     all-purpose flour
     water

Lay strips of bacon in a 10-quart soup pot and fry. Set bacon aside. To the bacon fat add flour and brown; then add the water. Add the crabs, onions and salt and pepper to taste. Add potatoes and cook for 1 hour.

While the crabs are cooking, make the dumplings. After 1 hour, take the potatoes and half of the crabs out of the pot and set aside. Cook the dumplings on top of the remaining crabs for 10 minutes with the lid on. Take the dumplings and remaining crabs out of the pot and thicken the gravy with a mixture of flour and

water to desired consistency. Return all the crabs and potatoes to the gravy, add the dumplings and bring up to heat. Serve hot.

Serves 4 to 6.

DUMPLINGS
1½ **cups all-purpose flour**
  2 **teaspoons baking powder**
 ¼ **teaspoon salt**
 ½ **teaspoons mixed dried herbs (parsley, thyme)**
  1 **tablespoon finely chopped onion**
  4 **tablespoons butter**
 ½ **cup milk, approximately**

Sift flour, baking powder and salt into a bowl. Stir in herbs and onion. Rub butter into dry ingredients until mixture resembles coarse breadcrumbs. Add enough milk to make a soft dough. Drop by spoonfuls on top of crabs as described.

*O*de to the crab:

    ... *Legend say he's a present/lesson*
    Directly from the Creator
    Crabmeat lovers learn
    The best things come
    In small and hard packages—
    Sometimes leg by leg.

                    LYNNE HAAS

Photograph by Melissa G. Dole, Maryland Watermen's Association

OLD BAY CRAB ARTICHOKE DIP

🦀 *This recipe by Chef Andrew Libertini was a favorite in the Chesapeake Bay Maritime Museum's Best Ever Crab Recipe Contest in 1997.*

1	**pound jumbo lump crabmeat**
¼	**cup mayonnaise**
¼	**cup sour cream**
¼	**cup cream cheese**
1	**teaspoon lemon juice**
2	**tablespoons Old Bay seasoning**
2	**tablespoons capers (rinsed)**
1	**jerk hot sauce**
1	**pack California Onion Dip/Soup Mix, crushed**
1	**small jar marinated artichoke hearts, quartered**
1	**French baguette, sliced, toasted lemon wedges and parsley**

Mix mayonnaise, sour cream, cream cheese, lemon juice, Old Bay seasoning, and hot sauce. Add dip mix, capers, and artichoke hearts. Fold crabmeat into wet mixture. Place in shallow baking dish and bake at 450°F for 8 to 10 minutes or until golden brown. Sprinkle with Old Bay seasoning. Garnish and serve with sliced toasted baguette.

Makes 2 pounds of dip.

Photograph by Melissa G. Dole, Maryland Watermen's Association

As we pull alongside the first floating buoy, the worker snags it with a boat hook. He places the float on the side rail (washboard) and runs the line attached to the submerged pot into a 12-inch disc winder that, when he steps on a pedal on the deck, reels the line and pot toward the boat. Once the pot is free of the surface, he lifts it over a five-foot stainless steel roller attached to the side of the boat in front of the winder disc, grabs the pot, and empties the crabs.

178

CATFISH CROWNED WITH CRABMEAT

Since catfish take on the taste of the water in which they live, I always use farm-raised catfish. Modern cultivation methods ensure fish that have a firm texture and sweet taste and that are cleaner than the ones pulled out of muddy waters and streams.

1	tablespoon butter
¼	cup minced green onion
3	tablespoons heavy cream
8	ounces crabmeat
1	teaspoon salt
	freshly ground pepper
4	catfish fillets (4 ounces each)
½	cup cornbread crumbs

Heat the butter in a skillet. Add the onions and sauté over medium heat until they are limp. Add the heavy cream and simmer, stirring occasionally, until thickened. Remove the pan from the heat. Fold the crabmeat into the onions and cream, then add salt and pepper to taste. Top each fillet with one-fourth of the mixture and spread it into an even layer. Sprinkle with cornbread crumbs. Place the fillets in a lightly buttered baking dish and bake at 350°F until fish flakes, about 15 minutes.

Serves 4.

Butch Cornelus and his crew near the end of their day of tending crab pots on the Potomac River near St. George Island.

Photograph by Bryan Hatchett

CRAB AND FLAT BEER OMELET

🦀 *The question of how to make a perfect omelet is often made to seem even more complicated than the origin of its name. But an omelet pan is the perfect way to begin. With shallow, sloping sides, a flat bottom and long handle, it's designed for easy movement, turning and removal of the omelet. Omelet pans range from 6 to 10 inches in diameter and can be made of aluminum, plain or enameled cast iron or stainless steel. Many of today's omelet pans have nonstick finishes.*

4   **slices crusty bread**
1   **cup flat beer**
1   **dozen eggs, well beaten**
8   **ounces crabmeat**
1   **stick butter**
1   **cup diced Gruyère cheese**

Cut bread into small pieces. Pour beer over the bread and let it stand until the bread is well softened. Beat the bread into the eggs. Heat butter in a large omelet pan, add crabmeat, pour in the egg mixture and top with Gruyère cheese. Cook over low heat until the bottom is just set. Brown the top lightly under the broiler and slide the omelet onto a heated plate for serving.

Serves 4.

Photograph by Marion E. Warren, from *The Flavor of the Chesapeake Bay Cookbook*

A trotline is a long line, resting on the Bay's bottom and anchored at both ends, to which a series of baits are tied at 3-foot intervals and worked from a boat. Commercial crabbers of the Severn River near Annapolis, Maryland, run one, two, or three lines up to a mile in length.

180

ALLENS FRESH SEAFOOD ASSEMBLY

🦀 *Each pita round splits horizontally to form a pocket into which a wide variety of ingredients can be stuffed to make a sandwich. This dish is best set off by a classic oak-aged Chardonnay such as the 1992 Beaulieu Vineyard Carneros Reserve Chardonnay from California.*

8	ounces crabmeat
1	small cooked lobster tail, chopped
6	tablespoons mayonnaise
¼	cup plain yogurt
½	teaspoon grated lemon rind
¼	cup sliced green onion
½	cup seeded and diced ripe tomato
1	tablespoon finely chopped fresh cilantro
	dash of Tabasco sauce
6	whole-wheat pita breads (1-ounce each)
6	small pieces leaf lettuce

In a small bowl, combine crabmeat, lobster, mayonnaise, yogurt, lemon rind, green onion, tomato, cilantro and Tabasco sauce. Cover and refrigerate until thoroughly chilled.

Carefully split each pita bread around about ⅓ of its circumference. Insert lettuce leaf and fill with ½ cup crabmeat mixture. Serve immediately.

Serves 6.

*T*he day's catch fresh off the workboat is heaped into bushel baskets. The worker is well aware that the frisky crustaceans will scurry "every whichaway." A simple remedy is to cut the bottom half out of a bushel basket and flip it over the top of another.

181

DAMIEN HEANEY'S BAKED GARLIC CRABS

🦀 *Just like tomatoes love basil, garlic loves crabs, and nowhere is this more true than in this recipe by executive chef Damien Heaney of Legends Restaurant in downtown Salisbury, Maryland.*

    1   dozen fresh crabs
    1   pound melted butter
   20   cloves garlic, whole
    1   cup chopped fresh parsley
        juice of 2 lemons
    2   crushed bay leaves
    1   teaspoon crushed dried thyme
    1   teaspoon crushed dried basil
    1   tablespoon seafood seasoning

Clean and split crabs in half and set aside. Melt butter; do not burn. Add garlic, parsley, lemon juice, bay leaves, thyme, basil, and seafood seasoning and simmer for 5 minutes. Pour over the crabs and marinate them for 2 hours. Pour the entire mixture into a flat baking pan and bake at 300° for approximately 30 minutes, basting occasionally with the garlic butter mixture. Serve hot with crab knives and plenty of napkins.

Serves 4.

*P*ictured here is a workman loading a crab cooker at E.J. Conrad and Sons Seafood Market in Mollusk, Virginia. The market's location on Greenvale Creek off the Rappahannock River is one of the nicest in all of Bay Country. Above the market is the Upper Deck Restaurant, whose seafood buffet is spectacular.

SOUFFLÉ PUFF WITH CRAB SAUCE

🦀 *The puff in this soufflé begins with a thick egg yolk-based sauce that is lightened with stiffly beaten egg whites. The real flavor comes with the addition of the crab sauce. M-m-m-m!*

3	tablespoons butter
4	tablespoons all-purpose flour
1	cup milk
2	teaspoons sugar
¼	teaspoon salt
2	eggs yolks, slightly beaten
2	egg whites
1	cup sour cream
	Crab Sauce (recipe follows)

Melt the butter in a sauce pan, add the flour and cook until the mixture bubbles. Add milk, stirring constantly, and cook until sauce is thickened. Reduce heat and cook for 5 minutes. Add sugar and salt. Add a small amount of the mixture to the egg yolks and mix well. Add the egg yolk mixture to the remaining sauce and beat thoroughly. Beat egg whites until stiff and fold into the mixture. Line an 8 x 12-inch baking dish with waxed paper. Butter and flour the waxed paper and pour in the egg mixture. Bake at 325°F for 35 minutes. Spread with Crab Sauce and top with sour cream.

Serves 6.

CRAB SAUCE

2	tablespoons butter
8	cooked shrimp, chopped
8	ounces crabmeat
2	cups white sauce (see page 173)
3	tablespoons sherry

Sauté the shrimp and crabmeat in butter. Add the white sauce and stir in the sherry.

*O*nce the crabs have completed the cooking cycle, they are left to cool until they can be handled, then delivered to the crab pickers.

183

PRIDE OF THE SHORE CREAMED CRAB

🦀 *In this version, creamed crabmeat is tossed onto toast rounds. Use a 3-inch cookie cutter to cut the rounds. Sliced tomatoes and corn on the cob complete the meal, and I like to crown this menu with homemade strawberry shortcake.*

2   slices bacon
1   stick butter
2   teaspoons cider vinegar
1   pound lump crabmeat
1   teaspoon all-purpose flour
½   cup half-and-half
     salt and freshly ground black pepper
1   teaspoon seafood seasoning
8   toast rounds
     crumbled bacon

In a large frying pan, fry bacon until crisp. Drain on paper towels and crumble. Remove the drippings from the pan and melt the butter. Add vinegar and crabmeat and sauté until well combined and heated through. Sprinkle flour over all and, stirring constantly, add half and half and stir to thicken. Add salt and pepper to taste and seafood seasoning. Serve over toast rounds. Garnish with crumbled bacon.

Serves 4.

"Maryland is for crabs" and "Virginia is for lovers." If that's the case, then the Chesapeake Bay must be for "crab lovers"!

CRAB COCKTAIL

🦀 *This cocktail, with its warming sauce, is a great first course or light meal for those hot, lazy days of summer. It's so easy to prepare that you'll probably want to fix it often. It's a perfect celebratory dish.*

    lettuce
1   pound lump crabmeat
    cocktail sauce
    parsley
    lemon wedges
    Cocktail Sauce (recipe below)

Arrange lettuce in 6 cocktail glasses. Place crabmeat on top and cover with cocktail sauce. Garnish with parsley and lemon wedges.
    Serves 6.

COCKTAIL SAUCE
¾ cup ketchup
¼ cup fresh lemon juice
3 tablespoons chopped celery
½ teaspoon salt
6 drops Tabasco sauce
   dash of cayenne pepper

Combine all ingredients and chill.

*A*s soon as I saw this yellow sign announcing hard blue crabs, I turned on Black Mallard Way and spent a little green. Color me happy.

"THE QUEEN IS IN" CRAB AND CORN BISQUE

🦀 *Hybrid Silver Queen is America's most beloved white corn, boasting uniform size, sweetness and quality. The ears grow 8 to 9 inches long and have 14 to 16 rows of creamy kernels. I believe that the southern Maryland area, between the Potomac and Patuxent Rivers, is where it grows best. So look for signs that read "The Queen is in."*

6	**ears fresh Silver Queen Corn**
1	**stick butter**
½	**cup all-purpose flour**
6	**green onions, chopped**
1	**quart chicken stock, hot**
1	**quart half-and-half**
1½	**tablespoons salt**
½	**teaspoon ground white pepper**
1	**pound crabmeat**

Cut the kernels from the ears of corn and set aside. Toss out the cobs. Melt the butter in a large saucepan and blend in the flour. Cook for about 3 minutes, stirring constantly. Add the chopped green onions and continue stirring until the onions soften, about 3 minutes longer. Whisk in the hot stock and bring the mixture to a boil. Add the half-and-half and the corn kernels. Season with salt and white pepper. Bring to a boil again and then simmer for about 20 minutes, or until the liquid is reduced to about 1½ quarts. Gently fold in the crabmeat and adjust seasonings to taste. Heat for just a minute or two longer to heat the crab through.

Serves 8.

Crisfield lawn furniture. This lawn in Crisfield, Maryland, is piled high with crab pots awaiting the first day of crab season.

CHAPTER 9
Crabby People

Photograph by JoAnn Dashiell

BOILED NOODLES WITH CRABMEAT SAUCE

Don't be confused by the term "Chinese cabbage." Although I know full well it can be confusing, the reason is that there are about six different names for this group of vegetables. I look for napa cabbage when I want to prepare this dish. Unlike the strong-flavored, waxy leaves on round heads of cabbage, the leaves of napa are crisp and delicately mild.

10	ounces egg noodles
1	teaspoon salt
3	tablespoons olive oil
2	onions, chopped
1	cup chopped Chinese cabbage
1	pound crabmeat
2	cups chicken stock
2	teaspoons cornstarch
2	teaspoons cold water
1	cup chopped watercress
2	teaspoons soy sauce

Boil noodles in salted water for 8 minutes. Drain and keep warm. Heat oil, brown onions and add Chinese cabbage. Add crabmeat and chicken stock and simmer for 10 minutes. Add cornstarch dissolved in cold water. Stir until thickened. Add chopped watercress and soy sauce and serve over hot noodles.

Serves 6.

Briggs White, pictured here, has thoughts on just one thing: dismantling the blue crab. A charter member of the Chesapeake Crab Eaters Society, Briggs takes great pride in the fact that when he's finished picking, you can't find enough meat in his discard pile to make a crab cake.

188

SHADYSIDE STIR-FRY

The concept of the stir-fry is simple: Quickly fry small pieces of food in a large pan over very high heat while constantly and briskly stirring. This technique requires a minimum amount of fat and results in food that is crisp and tender.

2	tablespoons olive oil
3	cloves garlic, minced
1	piece ginger (1 inch), peeled and minced
1	small red bell pepper, julienned
1	carrot, peeled and julienned
2	tablespoons soy sauce
1	can (3 ounces) sliced water chestnuts
1	package (10 ounces) frozen peas, thawed
8	ounces crabmeat
3	scallions, thinly sliced
¼	teaspoon salt
½	teaspoon pepper
¼	cup toasted coconut

In a large skillet, heat olive oil over medium-high heat until hot. Add garlic, ginger, bell pepper, and carrot. Stir-fry until slightly tender, about 3 minutes. Stir in soy sauce, water chestnuts, and peas and stir-fry until heated through, 1 to 2 minutes.

Add crabmeat, scallions, salt, and pepper. Toss and stir over medium-high heat until scallions are slightly wilted and all ingredients are heated through, about 2 minutes. Serve hot, garnished with toasted coconut.

Serves 3

*M*att Schmidt proudly displays two of the first crabs of summer. Matt explains how he attacks a crab: "... First I flip open the apron and flip off the top shell, then I pull the gills or devil's fingers out and toss them aside. The yellow stuff in the middle is the mustard. Actually, it's fat, but I love it. I also check out the points of the crabshell—there are some tasty tidbits there. I break the body in half and then remove the legs and claws one by one. Twist them as you pull and you'll get some large hunks of meat. Take your knife and split each half of the crab through horizontally, which exposes the chambers of crabmeat. Enjoy!"

189

CRABBIES

🦀 *Debbie Holland of New Church, Virginia, was a runner-up at the 1998 Crab Day Festival. Debbie's delightful "Crabbies" provide the perfect answer to those with busy schedules and hectic lifestyles. Crabbies can be prepared ahead, they freeze well and cook quickly.*

2	**sticks margarine, softened**
8	**ounces cold pack cheese, softened**
2	**tablespoons salad dressing**
2	**teaspoons Old Bay seasoning**
1	**teaspoon garlic salt**
1	**pound crabmeat**
12	**English muffins**

Mix all ingredients except English muffins. Split muffins and spread with crabmeat mixture. Broil until bubbly.

Serves 24.

*B*arbara Stewart, one of the crabbiest people I know, shows off her crab apron, crab nose, crab hat and crab T-shirt at the Chesapeake Bay Maritime Museum's annual Crab Day Festival.

Plum Creek Crab Salad

🦀 *This is a wonderfully light and refreshing summer dish to serve with a selection of freshly picked lettuce. Use basil leaves in clusters to garnish. It's magic!*

2 **ounces salad greens**
8 **ounces crabmeat**
16 **jumbo shrimp, cooked, shelled and deveined**
   basil leaf clusters

DRESSING

5 **large cloves garlic, unpeeled**
1 **large, ripe avocado**
4 **tablespoons sour cream**
5 **tablespoons olive oil**
2 **tablespoons lemon juice**
   salt and freshly ground black pepper

Dressing: Place garlic in a small saucepan of boiling water and simmer for 20 minutes, then drain and peel. Place the garlic, along with the remaining dressing ingredients, into a food processor and blend until smooth.

Salad: Divide the salad greens among four serving plates and arrange the crabmeat and shrimp on top. Drizzle dressing over each salad and serve immediately.

Serves 4.

*M*iss Alice Palmer picks crabs with the dexterity of a great artisan on Crab Day at the Chesapeake Bay Maritime Museum, St. Michaels, Maryland, 1997.

BECKY'S CRISPY FRIED SOFT-SHELL CRABS

The sight of these crisp fried crabs in a golden crust is sure to bring gasps of appreciation from your dinner guests. The soft crabs cook up in blankets of frothy egg whites and flour, leaving a succulent and quite delicious crab underneath.

3	egg whites
1½	cups all-purpose flour
1	teaspoon salt
1	teaspoon pepper
	vegetable oil for frying
12	soft-shell crabs

In a medium bowl, beat egg whites and ¼ cup water with a fork until frothy. In a large, shallow bowl, combine flour, salt, and pepper. In a large skillet, heat 2 inches oil to 375°F. Dip crabs in egg whites and drain off excess. Dredge in flour mixture. Working in batches, fry crabs, turning occasionally, until golden brown and crispy, 3 to 5 minutes. Drain on paper towels and serve hot.

Serves 4.

*B*ecky Cornelius, of Piney Point, Maryland, has a trained eye and can tell when crabs are about to shed. Soft-shell crabs are in peak condition for only about four hours, so they have to be tended several times a day. I was able to take a dozen home with me, and I don't think I've ever had better.

REHEARSAL DINNER CRAB

🦀 *A patty shell is usually made of puff pastry shaped into a cup. In this recipe, the shell is used to hold a delicate creamed crab mixture. Fresh patty shells are available in bakeries, while frozen, unbaked shells can usually be found in supermarkets.*

- ½ cup grated Swiss cheese
- 3 ounces cream cheese
- 3 tablespoons unsalted butter
- ½ cup milk
- 1¼ cup half-and-half
- 1 teaspoon dry mustard
- ⅛ teaspoon white pepper
- ⅛ teaspoon nutmeg
- 1 teaspoon salt
- 1 heaping teaspoon horseradish
- 1 slice white bread, crusts removed, broken into tiny pieces
- ¼ cup sherry
- 1 pound backfin crabmeat
- 6 patty shells

In a double boiler, melt Swiss cheese, cream cheese, and butter. Add milk slowly, and then add half-and-half. Thoroughly mix in dry mustard, white pepper, nutmeg, salt and horseradish; then add bread and sherry. Use a whisk to blend well. Cook until slightly thick. At the last minute, add the crabmeat. Use a spoon to stir it in gently, only long enough to make sure all of the crabmeat is warm. Serve over patty shells.

Serves 6.

*B*etsy Hedeman, of Relay, Maryland, impressed all of the judges at the 1998 Best Ever Crab Recipe Contest held at the Chesapeake Bay Maritime Museum's Annual Crab Day Festival. She invented this recipe for her daughter's wedding rehearsal dinner.

193

THE ULTIMATE SOFT-SHELL SANDWICH

🦀 *Soft-shell crabs are frightening to many, but "first fright, then delight"! Around Bay Country during the summer months, fried "softs" can be found on the menu of virtually every restaurant, from fine dining establishments to crab shanties—not to mention neighborhood kids sitting on front stoops munching white bread soft-shell sand-wiches with the crab legs dangling out over the edges. It doesn't get any better!*

6	strips bacon
1	cup bacon drippings
½	cup all-purpose flour
1	tablespoon cornmeal
1	teaspoon Old Bay seasoning
½	teaspoon black pepper
3	soft-shell crabs
6	slices rye bread
	Dijon mustard
3	large lettuce leaves
3	large tomato slices

In a skillet, fry the bacon and leave the drippings in the pan. Mix the flour, cornmeal, Old Bay seasoning, and black pepper in a shallow pan. Dredge the crabs one at a time in this mixture. Heat the bacon drippings on medium-high until flour dropped on the surface bubbles to the top. Fry the crabs on both sides until golden brown. Drain on paper towels.

Spread the rye bread slices with Dijon mustard, then layer on lettuce, tomato, bacon and crab.

Serves 3.

Lillian Brown of Annapolis, Maryland, had me begging for more. Her ultimate soft-shell sandwich is one of the reasons I love being a judge at the many crab cooking contests held around Bay Country. I tasted Lillian's sandwich at the Best Ever Crab Recipe Contest held at the Chesapeake Bay Maritime Museum, and to this day, every time I smell bacon frying I look for soft-shell crabs and rye bread.

PAN-FRIED ROCKFISH TOPPED WITH CRABMEAT

The firm-fleshed rockfish is suitable for virtually any cooking method. When I combine crabmeat with rockfish, I prefer to bake it or pan-fry it—either way, it's delicious.

- 1   cup all-purpose flour
- 1   tablespoon salt
- 1   tablespoon pepper
- 1   tablespoon paprika
- 2   fillets of rockfish (4 ounces each)
- ½   cup olive oil
- 1   cup fresh spinach
- ½   cup sliced onion
- 2   ounces diced Smithfield ham
- ¼   cup white wine
- ½   cup heavy cream
- ½   teaspoon seafood seasoning
      salt and pepper
- 4   ounces jumbo lump crabmeat

In a flat pan, mix flour, 1 tablespoon salt, 1 tablespoon pepper, and paprika and dredge rockfish fillets in the mixture. Pan fry in the olive oil and set aside. Add spinach, onion and ham to the pan and sauté lightly. Add white wine, cream, seafood seasoning, and salt and pepper to taste. Bring to a boil and then simmer until mixture is reduced to sauce consistency. Add crabmeat and simmer gently until heated through. Pour over rockfish and serve hot.

Serves 2.

*A*rlene Grauer was a great friend of the Chesapeake Bay. Her love for everything crabby—the food, the water, and the people. I'm sure that if Saint Peter has a gift shop at the pearly gates, she'll be there helping out.

195

CRABMEAT AU GRATIN SHARPTOWN

🦀 *Around Bay Country, two table condiments can be found in almost every kitchen: Worcestershire sauce and Tabasco sauce. Did you know that Worcestershire sauce was developed in India by the British and was named after the place it was first bottled, Worcester, England?*

CURRY SAUCE:

3½   **cups milk**
4   **tablespoons butter**
   pinch of curry powder
¼   **cup all-purpose flour**
½   **teaspoon Worcestershire sauce**
¼   **teaspoon salt**
   dash of Angostura bitters

CRABMEAT:

1½   **pounds crabmeat**
1   **cup breadcrumbs**
3   **tablespoons melted butter**

Curry Sauce: Scald milk in a medium saucepan; keep warm. heat butter and curry powder in a large, heavy saucepan over medium-low heat until curry is fragrant, 1 to 2 minutes; do not boil or curry will burn. Add flour and stir for 3 minutes. Slowly blend in hot milk. Add Worcestershire sauce, salt and Angostura bitters. Increase heat and bring to a boil, stirring. Reduce heat to low and cook for 5 minutes, stirring occasionally.

Crabmeat: Preheat broiler. Butter six small gratin dishes. Combine crabmeat and Curry Sauce. Divide among prepared dishes. Combine breadcrumbs and melted butter in a small bowl. Sprinkle evenly over the crabmeat and broil until crumbs are golden brown.

Serves 6.

Photograph by Bryan Hatchett

This is crab picker Lucinda Parker of Graham and Rollins Seafood in Hampton, Virginia. No one has ever figured out how to pick crabmeat mechanically as well or as thoroughly as hand pickers do it. Lucinda, who has been picking crabs for years, really knows how to remove all the pieces of shell, and she takes pride in her work—just look at those jumbo lumps!

CRAB-STUFFED POTATOES

Today hundreds of varieties of potatoes are grown worldwide. The one I like best for this dish is the russet. It's long, slighly rounded and has a rough brown skin. Its low moisture and high starch content make it perfect for stuffing, and when you stuff it with crab, it's heavenly.

4   large baking potatoes
2   egg yolks
      half-and-half
**4   tablespoons minced fresh parsley,
         divided**
2   tablespoons chopped fresh chives
1   cup crabmeat
½   cup grated Cheddar cheese.

Place the potatoes in a baking pan. Bake at 375°F for 1 hour or until tender. Remove the potatoes, but do not turn off the oven. Cut a thin slice from one side of each potato and scoop out the pulp, leaving a firm shell. Reserve the shells. Place the pulp in a medium-size mixer bowl, add the egg yolks and beat with an electric mixer until smooth. Beat in enough half & half to make the mixture light and fluffy. Fold in 2 tablespoons of the parsley, the chives, and the crabmeat, and then spoon the mixture into the reserved shells and sprinkle with the cheddar cheese. Return to the baking pan and bake about 20 minutes longer or until the cheese is melted and golden. Sprinkle with the remaining parsley.
    Serves 4.

This is Wilson Roe, professional crab net maker. Wilson began repairing fish nets when he was in high school. He saw the need for handmade crab nets and has perfected the art of making them over the past 50 years. Wilson is one of those people who make the Chesapeake area the special place it is.

197

OYSTER HOUSE ROAD CRAB PUFF

🦀 *Not only is this crab puff easy to eat, it's also easy to prepare. It's a truly delicious combination of flavors and one of my favorite dishes.*

6   **slices white bread, trimmed and cut into small cubes**
1   **pound crabmeat**
1   **cup grated Cheddar cheese**
4   **tablespoons melted butter**
3   **eggs**
2   **cups milk**
½   **teaspoon salt**
½   **teaspoon seafood seasoning**
½   **teaspoon dry mustard**

In a buttered 2-quart casserole, arrange bread cubes, crabmeat and cheese in layers. Top with melted butter. Beat eggs with milk, salt, mustard, and seafood seasoning and pour over casserole. Bake at 350°F until golden and puffy, about an hour.

Serves 4.

Here we find Briggs White on the left and Ron White on the right, both too puffed to pop. Briggs, Ron and I had just enjoyed steamed crabs and crab cakes at Stoney's Seafood House, Broomes Island, Maryland, along the banks of the Patuxent River.

MOUNT HOLLY BAKED CRAB

🦀 *Baked crab is a popular entrée for a dinner party, and the house smells wonderful as it is cooking. Rich and elegant, this dish only needs a fresh garden salad to complete the meal. Garnish your table with the ripest fruits of the season— berries, peaches or citrus slices.*

2 **cups milk**
1 **tablespoon all-purpose flour**
1 **tablespoon butter, softened**
½ **pound cheddar cheese, grated, divided**
1 **pound crabmeat**
½ **teaspooon seafood seasoning**
   salt and pepper
½ **cup fresh breadcrumbs**
2 **tablespoons butter**

In a large saucepan, bring milk to a boil. Cream the flour and 1 tablespoon butter together, add to the milk, and boil for 5 minutes, stirring constantly. Add half the Cheddar cheese, crabmeat, seafood seasoning and salt and pepper to taste. Spoon the mixture into a buttered baking dish and dot with 2 tablespoons butter, the breadcrumbs, and the remainder of the cheddar cheese. Bake at 350°F until golden brown, about 20 minutes.

Serves 6.

Like Boston, Massachusetts, Chestertown Maryland, celebrates its annual Tea Party. The event is held Memorial Day weekend, and I snapped this photo as the Kent County Band marched to the Chester River to join in the 1995 celebration.

199

LOONEY LEMON BAKED CRAB

A visit to the Cheshire Crab, Pasadena, Maryland, resulted in my eating another dozen crabs as well as a platter of freshly shucked oysters and clams on the half shell. That's when I spotted these waitresses getting ready for work.

This baked crab begins with a roux—a simple blend of flour and butter heated until the flour is cooked. In this dish the roux is cooked until it takes on a light brown color.

2	tablespoons all-purpose flour
3	tablespoons butter
1	cup light cream at room temperature
⅛	teaspoon allspice
½	teaspoon cayenne pepper
⅛	teaspoon nutmeg
1	teaspoon dry mustard
1	teaspoon seafood seasoning
1	lemon, seeded and finely chopped, peel included, pith removed
1	pound crabmeat
2	teaspoons Worcestershire sauce paprika
1	tablespoon butter

Brown flour in 3 tablespoons butter. Slowly add the cream, stirring continuously, and cook over low heat until thickened, but do not boil. Add allspice, cayenne pepper, nutmeg, dry mustard, seafood seasoning, lemon, crabmeat, and Worcestershire sauce and mix well. Spoon into a buttered baking dish. Sprinkle with paprika and dot with butter. Bake at 350°F for about 20 minutes.

Serves 6.

HACK NECK PANNED CRAB

The shallot, a small variety of onion that grows in clusters, is probably the most highly prized member of the onion family for Chesapeake cooks. Each clove is covered with a thin, papery skin. When choosing shallots, look for those that are dry-skinned, plump and firm, with no sign of wrinkling or sprouting. I'm a shallot lover and have used as many as six tablespoons of minced shallots when preparing panned crab.

- 4 **tablespoons butter**
- 2 **tablepoons finely chopped shallots**
- 1 **tablespoon finely chopped fresh parsley**
- ¼ **cup sherry**
  salt and freshly ground pepper
- 1 **pound crabmeat**
- ½ **cup pine nuts**
  rounds of fried toast
  chopped fresh parsley for garnish

In a skillet, heat the butter and sauté the shallots for 1 minute over medium heat. Add the parsley, sherry, and salt and pepper to taste. Immediately add the crabmeat and pine nuts and cook until just heated through, shaking the pan well. Spoon over toast rounds and serve with additional chopped parsley.

Serves 4.

Barb Kuebler and Connie Pehan celebrate at the 1998 Hard Crab Derby in Crisfield, Maryland. You can tell by the smiles on their faces that a good time was had by all.

201

LEGENDS RESTAURANT CRAB/POTATO PUFFS

Executive Chef Damien Heaney takes time from his busy schedule at Legends Restaurant in Salisbury, Maryland, to spin another yarn. Damien's expertise at using fresh herbs in his cookery is exceeded only by the beauty of his herb garden.

🦀 *These little puffs are some of the tastiest treats I've ever had, and just as Chef Damien suggested, I used small Red Bliss potatoes. They were oh, so tender and full of flavor. If you so desire, put the potatoes in a pastry bag and pipe them in mounds onto a buttered cookie sheet.*

1	tablespoon butter
½	teaspoon celery seed
⅛	teaspoon ground black pepper
1	teaspoon salt
2	cups hot mashed Red Bliss potatoes
2	egg yolks
¼	cup milk
8	ounces crabmeat
	chopped fresh parsley

Add butter, celery seed, black pepper and salt to the mashed potatoes and mix until the butter has melted. Beat the egg yolks and milk, add to the potatoes, and mix well. Drop potato mixture from a tablespoon in mounds onto a buttered cookie sheet, and with the back of the spoon make a depression in each puff. Fill the depressions with crabmeat and bake the puffs at 450°F until the potatoes are flecked with brown, about 10 minutes.

Serves 6.

JACK'S POINT CRAB RISE

🦀 *I've found that when making this crab rise, there's always some cheese sauce left over. No need to worry—it's a good base for a spaghetti sauce. In fact, you can make a sauce for any kind of pasta out of almost anything edible—honest! All that's required is that it have good flavor and be moderately thick. This should be a challenge for the imaginative cook!*

3	tablespoons butter
3	small shallots, finely chopped
3	tablespoons all-purpose flour
3	tablespoons tomato paste
½	cup heavy cream
1	teaspoon salt
½	teaspoon freshly ground black pepper
½	teaspoon cayenne pepper
1	teaspoon dried tarragon
2	tablespoons brandy
4	egg yolks
6	egg whites
1	pound crabmeat
	Cheese Sauce (recipe follows)

In a saucepan, sauté the shallots in the butter until soft. Add the flour. Cook for 1 minute, stirring constantly. Add the tomato paste and cream and stir until smooth. Add salt, black pepper, cayenne pepper, tarragon and brandy. Stir in the egg yolks and beat well. Beat the egg whites until firm but not stiff and fold into the mixture. Butter a 1½-quart soufflé dish. Place one-third of the crabmeat on the bottom. Add one-third of the soufflé mixture, then another third of the crab, another third of soufflé mixture, the last third of crab and the last third of the soufflé mixture. Bake at 375°F until puffy and golden, about 30 minutes. Serve with Cheese Sauce.

Serves 6.

CHEESE SAUCE

2	tablespoons butter
1	teaspoon finely grated onion
2	tablespoons all-purpose flour
1½	cups light cream
¾	cup grated cheddar cheese
	dash of Worcestershire sauce
	pinch of cayenne pepper
½	teaspoon paprika
	salt

In a saucepan, melt the butter over medium heat, add the onion, and cook only until the onion is golden. Stir in the flour and add the cream to make a cream sauce. Add the cheese, Worcestershire sauce, cayenne pepper, paprika and salt to taste and stir only until the cheese is melted.

Makes 2 cups.

*T*alk about crabby people, here are three of the crabbiest. On the left is Tom Knorr, chief cook, owner and bottle washer at the Red Roost Crabhouse in Whitehaven, Maryland. On the right is Russell Dashiell, Jr., widely known and esteemed Eastern Shore attorney. The last time I saw the guy in the middle he was walking sideways!

Photograph by JoAnn Dashiell

203

FORT STORY CRAB PUFFOUT

🦀 *A puffout must be taken to the table as soon as it's removed from the oven. The collar may be removed in the kitchen, but the puffout will begin to deflate. For this reason, you may choose to take it to the table with the collar still attached to the dish. Have a plate ready on which to place the foil and string, and remove the collar at the table with ceremony and flair.*

    4   tablespoons cup butter
    ½   cup all-purpose flour
    ⅛   teaspoon nutmeg
    ⅛   teaspoon pepper
        pinch of saffron
    2   cups milk
    1   cup shredded Swiss cheese
    8   ounces crabmeat
    6   egg yolks
    6   egg whites, beaten until stiff

Attach a foil collar to a 2-quart soufflé dish as follows: Measure enough foil to go around the dish plus 2-inch overlap. Fold foil in thirds lengthwise. Lightly butter one side of foil band. With buttered side in, position the foil around the dish, letting the collar extend 2½ inches above dish. Fasten with tape or a paper clip.

In a saucepan, melt butter. Stir in flour, nutmeg, pepper, and saffron. Add milk all at once. Cook and stir until thickened and bubbly. Cook 1 to 2 minutes more. Add Swiss cheese and stir until melted. Removed pan from heat and stir in crabmeat. In a small mixer bowl, beat egg yolks until thick and lemon-colored. Gradually add the crab/Swiss cheese mixture, stirring constantly. Cool slightly. Fold into egg whites and then turn into the prepared soufflé dish. Bake at 325°F until a knife inserted near the center comes out clean, 45 to 55 minutes. Serve immediately.

Serves 6.

Crabs sold for 50 cents a dozen on April 20, 1930. That was the day Connor Butler started cooking crabs at Popes Creek, Maryland. Popes Creek offered a ferry and train depot and the crab shack stood at the water's edge. Connor prepared crabs for the train and ferry passengers. He took their orders in the morning and would have the hot, spicy crabs ready for the commute home in the evening.

CRABMEAT TOPPED WITH PEPPERHASH

🦀 *Hash is a dish of finely chopped meat (roast beef and corned beef are the most common), potatoes and seasonings, usually fried together until lightly brown. Here, in this much lighter rendition of the time-honored dish, crabmeat is substituted for the meat.*

4   strips bacon, chopped
1   large onion, chopped
1   pound crabmeat
2   cups cubed boiled potatoes
2   tablespoons chopped fresh parsley
1   tablespoon freshly squeezed lemon
      juice
4   tablespoons heavy cream
      salt and cayenne pepper
4   poached eggs
      Pepperhash (recipe follows)

In a large skillet, cook the bacon until crisp. Remove from the pan. There should be about 2 tablespoons of drippings in the pan. If not, add a little olive oil. Add the onions and potatoes to the skillet and fry for 10 minutes, stirring frequently, until brown and crispy.

Add the crabmeat to the cooked bacon and then add parsley, lemon juice and cream. Combine well and season with salt and cayenne pepper. Continue to cook without stirring until bottom is crisp and golden brown. Turn onto a platter and top with poached eggs. Pass the Pepperhash.

Serves 4.

PEPPERHASH
2   green bell peppers, minced
2   red bell peppers, minced
⅛   teaspoon finely chopped chili pepper
1   large onion, finely chopped
¼   cup cider vinegar
1   teaspoon sugar
½   teaspoons salt
1   tablespoon fresh thyme sprigs
1   bay leaf

Place the chopped peppers and onions in a pot and cover with boiling water; let stand for 5 minutes. Drain, cover with boiling water again, and let stand for 10 minutes. Drain again. Add the vinegar, sugar, salt, thyme sprigs tied together, and bay leaf and bring to a boil. Cook, stirring occasionally, until the vegetables are just tender, about 15 minutes. Discard the thyme sprigs and bay leaf.

I took this picture of photographer Noel Schwab while he was on assignment near Crisfield, Maryland. Noel had found an old ladder and climbed up it to get a better view of this crab shanty and the surrounding waters.

205

CELERY RIBS STUFFED WITH CRAB

🦀 *The quickest and most thorough way to rid a celery rib of strings is to scrape it from top to bottom with a short-bladed knife.*

    8   ounces cream cheese at room
            temperature
    8   ounces crabmeat
    ½   teaspoon salt
        dash of cayenne pepper
   12   ribs celery

Combine cream cheese, crabmeat, salt and cayenne pepper. Wash and dry the celery and cut into desired lengths. Stuff with crab mixture and refrigerate until ready to serve.

Serves a crowd.

Chef Tim Wheatley of Buddy's Crab and Rib Restaurant at the City Dock, Annapolis, Maryland, proudly displays the day's catch. It consists of mussels, oysters, clams, blue crabs, crab legs and Maine lobsters. Lucky me!

CURRIED CRABMEAT WITH TOASTED ALMONDS

Did you know that authentic Indian curry powder is freshly ground each day and can vary dramatically depending on the region and the cook? Such curry powder is a pulverized blend of up to twenty spices, herbs and seeds.

- ½ cup slivered almonds
- 2 tablespoons olive oil
- 5 tablespoons butter
- ¼ cup finely chopped green onion
- ¼ cup finely chopped green pepper
- 1 tablespoon curry powder
- 1 teaspoon chili powder
- 1 pound crabmeat
- 1 cup heavy cream
- 1 teaspoon salt
- 4 cups cooked rice
- ¼ cup chopped fresh parsley

Place the almonds on an oiled baking sheet and toast at 350°F, stirring frequently, until lightly browned and crisp. Set aside to cool. Heat the olive oil and butter in a skillet, and when fairly hot, add the onion and green pepper. Let them cook for several minutes over medium heat. Add the curry powder and chili powder and mix well. When the pepper and onion are tender, add the crabmeat and toss until heated through. Add the cream and salt and blend well; cook through. If the crab absorbs too much cream and the mixture looks dry, add more cream. Put rice in a buttered 8-inch ring mold and unmold on a hot platter. Spoon the crab mixture into the center and top with the chopped parsley and toasted almonds.

Serves 6.

Leonard and Josephine Copsey are the proud owners of the Drift Inn, a southern Maryland tradition on the banks of the Patuxent River near Oraville, Maryland. The Drift Inn has been serving delicious, hot steamed crabs since 1953. The Copsey family takes pride in their cooked crab, served by one of their daughters or grandchildren.

COLONIAL BEACH CRAB CAKES

🦀 *Mace tastes and smells like a pungent version of nutmeg, and for a very good reason: mace is the membrane that covers the nutmeg seed. Use it sparingly.*

½ teaspoon dry mustard
1 teaspoon water
1 pound crabmeat
3 egg yolks
2 tablespoons mayonnaise
   fine dry breadcrumbs
2 teaspoons lemon juice
   dash of cayenne pepper
⅛ teaspoon ground mace
   salt
   flour
1 tablespoon cold water
   all-purpose flour for dredging
1 tablespoon butter
2 tablespoons salad oil

Mix the mustard with the 1 teaspoon water and let the mixture stand for 5 minutes. Add the mustard, crabmeat, 2 of the egg yolks, the mayonnaise, 5 teaspoons of the breadcrumbs, the lemon juice, cayenne pepper, mace and salt to taste. Mix the ingredients well, shape into 8 cakes, and chill for several hours.

Beat the remaining egg yolk with the 1 tablespoon water. Roll the cakes in flour, dip them in the egg yolk/water mixture, and then roll in breadcrumbs. Heat the butter and oil in a skillet, add the crab cakes, and brown quickly on both sides. Serve hot.

Serves 4.

*P*arker's Crab Shore in Colonial Beach, Virginia, is one of my favorite Bay tripping stops. On my latest visit, I snapped this photo of Shirley Jenkins making up another batch of her delightful crab cakes. I couldn't resist.

CHAPTER 10
Crabgrala

BARBECUED GRILLED CRABS

🦀 *When preparing these tasty grilled crabs, it is important to pay close attention to the intense heat that a grill can produce. Keep the crabs moving, basting as you go, so they won't dry out.*

6   hard-shell crabs
Barbecue Sauce (recipe follows)
melted butter

Crack open the crabs. Remove the gray gill matter (If the crabs are fat, there will be a great deal of yellow substance. This is edible and much prized.) Remove the claws and crack them without peeling. Marinate in barbecue sauce for at least 2 hours.

About a half hour before cooking, get the grill heated up. When ready, place crabs directly on the grill. Cook about 15 minutes on each side. Baste while cooking with leftover Barbecue Sauce. Serve with melted butter for dipping.

Serves 2.

BARBECUE SAUCE:
1   stick butter, melted
1   tablespoon fresh lemon juice
1   tablespoon shredded green onion
3   teaspoons liquid hickory smoke
3   teaspoons Worcestershire sauce
pinch of cayenne pepper

Mix all ingredients.

I spotted this stuffed crab at the Crab Soup Cook-off in Annapolis, Maryland. Where else but in Annapolis could you sample twenty different crab soups by some of the best chefs in Maryland for under $5.00?

VINTAGE CRAB IMPERIAL

🦀 *You've probably noticed that many recipes in this book contain sherry. Perhaps it's time to take a closer look at it. Fortified wines like port and sherry have very strong flavors, so caution is the byword when adding them to crab dishes. Always begin by adding just a little at a time, and then taste, taste, taste!*

2	tablespoons minced green pepper
2	tablespoons grated onion
5	tablespoons butter
1½	pounds lump crabmeat
2	tablespoons chopped fresh parsley
1	tablespoon dry sherry
	pinch of cayenne pepper
½	teaspoon seafood seasoning
½	cup heavy cream
	salt and freshly ground black pepper
½	cup fine dry breadcrumbs

Sauté the green pepper and onion in 2 tablespoons of the butter for a few minutes until soft. Mix the crabmeat, softened pepper and onion, parsley, sherry, cayenne pepper, seafood seasoning and cream. Season lightly with with salt and pepper.

Just before serving, preheat the oven to 450°F. Fry the breadcrumbs in the remaining butter over medium-high heat for a minute or so.

Butter ceramic baking shells. Mound the crab mixture in the shells, sprinkling the breadcrumbs over the top, and bake until the top is bubbling and golden brown, about 10 minutes. Serve immediately.

Serves 6.

Now you know why we call it "the land of pleasant living."

KING STREET CRAB GUMBO

*W*elcome to Crab Country, where the dishes hark back to the region's first settlers.

🦀 *Gumbo is a Creole specialty and a mainstay of New Orleans cuisine. It's a thick stew-like dish, and the reason I like to prepare it is that it can be made with a variety of ingredients—such as chicken, sausage, ham or shrimp—but my favorite version uses two pounds of crabmeat. It's fit for a king!*

4   tablespoons bacon drippings
6   tablespoons all-purpose flour
1   green pepper, chopped
1   rib celery, chopped
2   large onions, chopped
2   pounds okra, chopped
2   cups peeled, seeded and chopped
    tomatoes
2   small cans tomato paste
2   quarts chicken stock
2   pounds crabmeat
2   bay leaves
    salt and pepper to taste
6   cups cooked rice

Brown the flour in the bacon drippings over low heat. Add pepper, celery, onions and okra. Cook about 20 minutes, stirring constantly. Add tomatoes and tomato paste and mix well. In a large soup pot, add mixture to stock. Simmer gently for 1 hour. Add crabmeat and bay leaves and simmer half an hour more. Season with salt and pepper. Remove bay leaves before serving. Serve with rice.

Serves 12.

CRAB COVE RICE RING

🦀 *Instant or quick-cooking rice has been fully or partially cooked, then dehydrated. It only takes a few minutes to cook, but its flavor doesn't match that of regular rice. However, I like to use it in this dish because of its texture.*

1   **stick butter**
1   **pound crabmeat**
¾   **cup blanched, halved almonds**
    salt and freshly ground black pepper
½   **cup heavy cream**
3   **tablespoons chopped fresh parsley**
    rice ring

In a medium-size skillet, heat 4 tablespoons of the butter, add the crabmeat and toss lightly until delicately browned. Meanwhile, in a separate skillet, heat the remaining butter, add almonds and and cook over brisk heat until lightly browned. Add salt and pepper to taste, then stir in crabmeat. Add cream and parsley and bring mixture to a boil. Reduce heat and simmer for 2 minutes. Serve in a rice ring. I like to garnish this disk with a crispy fried soft-shell crab.

    Serves 4.

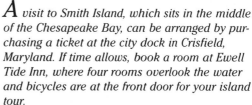

A visit to Smith Island, which sits in the middle of the Chesapeake Bay, can be arranged by purchasing a ticket at the city dock in Crisfield, Maryland. If time allows, book a room at Ewell Tide Inn, where four rooms overlook the water and bicycles are at the front door for your island tour.

BAKED CRAB À LA HEATHER

To bring out the flavor of sesame seeds, toast them either in a dry skillet over medium heat or in a 350° oven. Stir occasionally, toasting only until the seeds begin to turn golden brown.

2   **packages (10 ounces each) frozen spinach**
1¼   **cups sour cream, divided**
1   **pound crabmeat**
2   **cups toasted Italian bread croutons**
1   **stick butter, softened**
2   **tablespoons minced green onions**
2   **teaspoons minced fresh parsley**
     salt and freshly ground black pepper
     cayenne pepper
½   **cup toasted sesame seeds**

Cook and drain spinach and place it in a buttered casserole. Mix ¼ cup of the sour cream with the crabmeat and spread it over the spinach. Spread the croutons on top of the crabmeat. Mix butter, the remaining cup of sour cream, green onions, parsley, and salt, black pepper and cayenne pepper to taste. Spread this mixture over the croutons and sprinkle sesame seeds on top. Bake at 350°F for 30 minutes.

Serves 6.

This photo was taken around 1984 on Route 2 about halfway between Annapolis and Baltimore. In those days, crab trucks like Tony's Crab Pot appeared up and down the highway. Eventually, Tony extended his operation all the way to Miami. Why? Well, what's a fella to do when the urge for crabs strikes!

BLUEFISH STUFFED WITH CRABMEAT

This crabmeat stuffing imparts a marvelous flavor to the Bay's favorite—bluefish. When the limited bluefish season is over, this stuffing technique can be used with any firm fish.

- 1 **tablespoon minced onion**
- 1 **tablespoon minced fresh parsley**
- 3 **tablespoons butter, divided**
- 4 **slices white bread**
- 1 **pound crabmeat**
  - 2 **eggs**
- 1 **teaspoon seafood seasoning**
- 1 **tablespoon lemon juice**
- 8 **small, dressed whole bluefish**
  - **lemon wedges**

Sauté onion and parsley in 1 tablespoon of the butter. Add bread broken into small crumbs. Add crabmeat, eggs, seafood seasoning and lemon juice. The mixture will be dry and crumbly. Pack stuffing into the body cavities of the bluefish. Melt the remaining butter and brush fish with it. Bake at 350°F for 30 minutes or until fish flakes to the touch of a fork. Serve with lemon wedges.

Serves 8.

"The jukebox is important at a crab house. 'Country' (especially Travis Tritt, Conway Twitty, Mary Chapin Carpenter, and Willie Nelson) means the place has potential. Rock and roll and crabs doesn't work; however, some rockabilly, such as Carl Perkins, is just fine." Pat Piper, Chesapeake Bay Magazine, *July 1995.*

DRY DOCK CRABMEAT COCKTAIL

🦀 *In general, prepared mustard is made from powdered mustard, a liquid such as water, vinegar, wine or beer, and various seasonings. Mustards come in a wide variety of flavors and textures, from smooth to grainy and from very mild to scorching hot. When I prepare this crabmeat cocktail, I choose one that's very mild and adds its flavor rather than overpowering the dish.*

  3 **hard-boiled eggs (separate yolks and whites)**
  1 **tablespoon butter**
  1 **tablespoon prepared mustard**
½ **cup mayonnaise**
¼ **cup chili sauce**
¼ **cup red wine vinegar**
    pinch of sugar
¼ **cup whipped cream**
  1 **pound lump crabmeat**

Blend mashed egg yolks with butter. Add mustard, mayonnaise, chili sauce, vinegar, sugar, and whipped cream and mix well. Serve over crabmeat and garnish with chopped egg whites.
  Serves 6.

One of the things I like about this picture is that it captures a good feeling for the rural nature of Smith Island. There's nothing but marsh grass, dilapidated crab shanties and an occasional tree or two.

HELEN AND JOHN'S CRAB CAKES

"Don't even think of making these crab cakes without using 2-day-old hamburger buns." This warning was passed on to me by my brother-in-law John Gorden. *"And another thing—make sure that they sit in the refrigerator overnight. Otherwise you'll have a patty that will fall apart."* John was right.

2	2-day-old hamburger buns
1	pound lump crabmeat
1	tablespoon fresh parsley
½	cup (scant) mayonnaise
	shake of pepper sauce
1	tablespoon Old Bay seasoning
¼	teaspoon salt
1	tablespoon Worcestershire sauce
2	tablespoons water
1	tablespoons finely chopped onion
2	cups cornflake crumbs
	peanut oil for frying

Rub hamburger buns through your hands until very fine, and mix crumbs with the crabmeat. Mix parsley, mayonnaise, pepper sauce, Old Bay seasoning, salt, Worcestershire sauce, water and onion and add to crabmeat mixture. Form crabmeat mixture into 8 cakes and dredge in cornflake crumbs. Refrigerate overnight so cakes will set up.

Fry in oil until brown on both sides.
Serves 4.

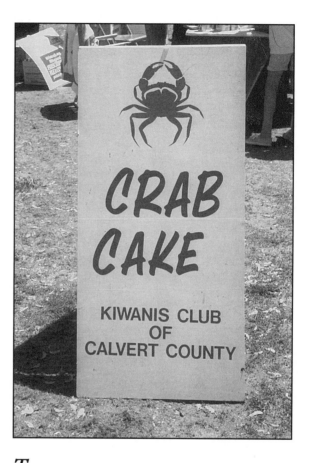

*T*he Kiwanis Club of Calvert County, Maryland, displayed this sign at the North Beach, Maryland annual Bayfest Celebration. It worked. Two to go, please!

217

GRACIE'S CRAB CHILE

*Y*ou can walk down almost any street in Baltimore, Maryland, and find a place to sit a while, sip a cold beer, and pick a steamed crab or two. When I saw this sign, I quickly took a picture and paid a visit to the Crab Alley bar. Is this living, or what?

🦀 *Salsa is the Mexican word for sauce and it can signify a cooked or fresh mixture. Salsa cruda is uncooked salsa.*

1	**pound cream cheese at room temperature**
1	**cup Mexican salsa cruda**
½	**cup mayonnaise**
1	**teaspoon chili powder**
½	**teaspoon Worcestershire sauce**
1	**pound lump crabmeat**
4	**drops Tabasco sauce**
¾	**cup finely crushed tortilla chips**

In a bowl, mix the cream cheese, salsa, mayonnaise, chili powder, and Worcestershire sauce. Fold in the crabmeat and season with Tabasco sauce. Transfer to a shallow 1-quart baking dish.

Sprinkle the top with the crushed tortilla chips. Bake at 350°F until bubbling, about 40 minutes. Serve warm with raw vegetables or tortilla chips for dipping.

Serves 6.

BAKED OYSTERS TOPPED WITH CRABMEAT

🦀 *Oysters Rockefeller was created at Antoine's Restaurant in New Orleans in the late 1890s. This popular dish was reportedly named for John D. Rockefeller because it is so rich. It is said that the rich get richer . . . see how rich this dish becomes when you top it with lump crabmeat. M-m-m!*

    rock salt
1   **stick butter, divided**
¼   **cup chopped green onions**
¼   **cup chopped celery**
1   **tablespoon dried chervil**
1   **tablespoon dried parsley flakes**
1   **cup loosely packed fresh watercress
      leaves plus additional sprigs for
      garnish**
⅓   **cup soft breadcrumbs**
⅛   **teaspoon salt**
    pinch of ground black pepper
    pinch of cayenne pepper
1   **package (10-ounce) frozen chopped
      spinach, thawed**
⅓   **cup Pernod**
2   **dozen fresh oysters on the half shell**
½   **cup freshly grated Parmigiano-Reggiano
      cheese**
8   **ounces lump crabmeat**

Sprinkle a layer of rock salt in two 15 x 10 x 1-inch jelly roll pans; set pans aside.

Melt ¼ cup of the butter in a large skillet over medium heat; add green onions, celery, chervil and parsley flakes, and cook, stirring constantly, until tender. Add watercress; stir until wilted and remove from heat. Pour mixture into the container of an electric blender; process for 1 minute, stopping once to scrape down sides. Stir in breadcrumbs, salt, black pepper and cayenne pepper.

Drain spinach well and press between paper towels to remove excess moisture. Melt the remaining ¼ cup butter in a skillet over medium heat, add spinach, and cook, stirring constantly, for 3 minutes; stir in watercress mixture and Pernod.

Scrub oyster shells and open, discarding tops. Arrange shell bottoms (containing oysters) over rock salt in jelly roll pans. Spoon 2 teaspoons watercress mixture over each oyster; sprinkle with crabmeat and Parmigiano-Reggiano cheese. Bake at 450°F for 6 to 8 minutes or until oysters begin to curl. Garnish with watercress sprigs.

Makes 2 dozen.

*A*ntiques and crabs—two of life's greatest pleasures.

SOFT CRABS WITH TOASTED MACADAMIA NUTS

"Hard crabs, soft crabs, even a shedder. I can take 'em home and eat 'em the sooner the better. I don't need a knife and I don't need a mallet, just a back creek crab to satisfy my palate."

Lyrics to "Back Creek Crab" by Jeff Holland

Pictured in photograph is Cindy Musterman.

🦀 *When choosing soft-shell crabs, it's a good idea to get to know your fishmonger. Insist on crabs that are alive. "If it ain't kicking, it ain't cooking," is my motto. Take a crab with little bubbles streaming from its mouth. If they're on ice, ask the seller to run his hands along the crabs on display . . . and choose the ones that move.*

8	soft-shell crabs
2	cups all-purpose flour
	small pinch of cayenne pepper
	salt and freshly ground pepper
1	cup milk
2	large eggs
	vegetable oil for frying
4	tablespoons unsalted butter
1	cup coarsely chopped unsalted macadamia nuts
2	tablespoons lime juice
1	lime sliced thin

Pat the crabs dry with paper towels. In a shallow dish, combine the flour with the cayenne pepper and salt and black pepper to taste. In another dish, beat the milk and eggs together. Dip each crab in the flour mixture to coat lightly, then into the milk mixture, and finally back into the flour again., shaking off excess flour. Place the crabs on a rack and refrigerate for 2 to 3 hours.

Preheat the oven to 200°F. Pour oil into a frying pan so it comes up the sides ¼ inch. Heat it over medium-high heat until hot but not smoking. Carefully add four crabs to the pan. Cook, turning once with tongs, until golden brown, 3 to 4 minutes. Transfer to a paper-towel-lined baking sheet and keep warm in the oven while you cook the remaining crabs.

Discard the oil from the frying pan. Melt the butter in the pan over medium heat. Add the macadamia nuts and cook until lightly browned, about 2 minutes. Remove from the heat and stir in the lime juice. Pour nut butter over the crabs and serve at once garnished with lime slices.

Serves 4.

REEDVILLE BROILED SOFT-SHELL CRABS

🦀 *Here are some hot tips from the McIlhenny Company, makers of Tabasco Pepper Sauce. Did you know that each two-ounce bottle of Tabasco Pepper Sauce contains at least 720 drops (60 drops per teaspoon)? Now let's see how many times I can prepare these Reedville broiled soft-shell crabs using just one bottle . . .*

- 8 **soft-shell crabs**
  flour for dredging
- 1 **teaspoon salt**
- 1 **teaspoon paprika**
- 24 **drops Tabasco sauce, divided**
- 1 **stick butter**
  Lemon Mayonnaise (recipe below)

Dredge the crabs lightly with flour and sprinkle with salt and paprika. Add 2 drops of Tabasco to each one and dot well with butter. Place in an oven-proof frying pan and broil 4 inches from the heat about 4 minutes on each side. When you turn them, dot well with butter again and sprinkle lightly with salt and Tabasco. Place on a hot platter and pour the pan juices over them. Serve with Lemon Mayonnaise.

Serves 4.

LEMON MAYONNAISE:
- ⅔ **cup mayonnaise**
- 2 **tablespoons light cream**
- 2 **teaspoons lemon juice**

In a small bowl, combine mayonnaise, cream, and lemon juice. Stir until well blended. Refrigerate.

Makes ⅔ cup.

*R*eedville, Virginia, is located where the Potomac River joins the Chesapeake Bay in the northern neck of Virginia. Reedville's main street was once known as "Millionaires' Row." The town was famous for the menhaden fish industry that was developed at the turn of the century. Not much fishing is done here today, but you'll find plenty of fat, juicy soft crabs.

221

MARIAN'S CRAB SPREAD

🦀 *Marian Margaret Hartnett was my mother's maiden name, and this was a crab dip she made often. If you're going to do what Mom always did, you might as well double the recipe. With four-teen little mouths to feed, Mom knew one was not enough. Depending on how many mouths you have to feed, you can double or even triple the recipe—it's that good.*

8 ounces cream cheese, softened
1 tablespoon heavy cream
1 pound lump crabmeat
2 tablespoons chopped onion
1 teaspoon prepared horseradish
½ teaspoon freshly ground black pepper
½ cup toasted almonds

Combine the cream cheese and heavy cream and then add the crabmeat, onion, horseradish, and pepper. Blend well and place in an oven-proof dish; sprinkle with toasted almonds. Bake for 15 minutes at 375°F. Serve hot with assorted crackers.

Serves 10.

Jenkins Creek, Maryland, at sunset, circa 1998.

CRABMEAT ALFRED

🦀 *Tarragon is a aromatic herb of the daisy family distinguished by narrow, pointed, dark green leaves with an anise-like flavor. Tarragon is widely used in classic French cooking for a variety of dishes including chicken and vegetables. Now see what it does for crab!*

⅓   **cup tarragon vinegar**
¼   **cup cider vinegar**
⅔   **cup extra virgin olive oil**
     dash of salt
     freshly ground black pepper to taste
1   **pound crabmeat**
     lemon wedges
     fresh tarragon leaves

Combine the vinegars, olive oil, salt and pepper in a small bowl. Whisk vigorously to form an emulsion (the oil and vinegar should not separate). Refrigerate, covered, for 2 days.

Place the crabmeat in a shallow dish, spoon the dressing over it, and serve immediately. Garnish with lemon wedges and fresh tarragon leaves.

Serves 6.

Some say a pot of gold lies at the end of every rainbow. Well, how about a pot of crabs? Jenkins Creek crab shanty, circa 1998.

SHERRIED LUMP CRAB WITH CORNMEAL CAKES

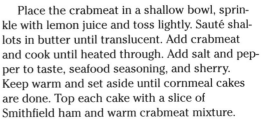 *I like to play with contrasts. In this recipe, I've paired Smithfield ham (salty), sherry (sweet), and cornmeal cakes (yummy) to meld with the crabmeat. It's a simple dish in which the delicate flavor of the crab shines.*

SHERRIED LUMP CRAB:
- 8 ounces lump crabmeat
- ½ teaspoon lemon juice
- 1 teaspoon minced shallot
- 3 tablespoons butter
  salt and pepper
- ½ teaspoon seafood seasoning
  dash of sherry
- 8 slices center cut Smithfield ham
  Cornmeal Cakes (recipe follows)

Place the crabmeat in a shallow bowl, sprinkle with lemon juice and toss lightly. Sauté shallots in butter until translucent. Add crabmeat and cook until heated through. Add salt and pepper to taste, seafood seasoning, and sherry. Keep warm and set aside until cornmeal cakes are done. Top each cake with a slice of Smithfield ham and warm crabmeat mixture.

Serves 4.

CORNMEAL CAKES:
- 2 cups milk
- ½ cup light cream
- 2 cups water
- 1 cup cornmeal
- 2 sticks butter, melted
- 2⅔ cups all-purpose flour
- 2 teaspoons baking powder
- 1 teaspoon baking soda
- 1 teaspoon salt
- 2 tablespoons sugar
- 3 eggs

Heat milk, cream and 2 cups water to boiling. Add cornmeal and whip until smooth. Cool; then add butter, flour, baking powder, baking soda, salt, sugar and eggs and beat well.

Using about ⅓ cup batter per cake, cook the cornmeal cakes as you would pancakes on a hot griddle, using just enough oil on the griddle to keep cakes from sticking.

I love the ingenuity that some people have. In today's world, when computer printouts are so easy, it's nice that some of us can take something like a paper plate and a clothespin and get someone else to react to it. My reaction was to go to the car to get my camera and purchase a pound of backfin for dinner and a can of crab claws to eat on the drive back home.

STUFFED CRABS WITH ALMOND BUTTER SAUCE

🦀 *Larousse defines sauces as "liquid seasoning for food." Webster, however, does more for the taste buds, listing sauce as "a condiment or composition of condiments and appetizing ingredients eaten with food as a relish." This almond butter sauce takes the definition to yet another level.*

6	cooked crabs, shells reserved
1	tablespoon butter
1	tablespoon all-purpose flour
1	cup milk
½	cup chopped onion
¼	cup chopped celery
½	teaspoon nutmeg
2	tablespoons fresh breadcrumbs
	Almond Butter Sauce (recipe below)

Pick the meat from the crabs and set aside. Melt 1 tablespoon butter and stir in the flour. Add milk slowly and cook, stirring constantly, until the mixture thickens. Add onion, celery, and nutmeg. Stir gently, add crabmeat, and again stir gently. Spoon the mixture into the reserved crab shells and top with breadcrumbs. Bake at 325°F until hot and bubbly, about 20 minutes. Top with Almond Butter Sauce.

Serves 6.

ALMOND BUTTER SAUCE:

2	tablespoons slivered almonds
1	stick butter, divided
2	tablespoons pimiento, drained and finely chopped
2	teaspoons finely chopped fresh parsley
2	teaspoons lemon juice
½	teaspoon salt

Sauté the almonds slowly in 2 tablespoons of the butter until golden brown. Cool. Cream the remaining butter and add the almonds, pimiento, parsley, lemon juice, and salt; mix thoroughly.

My first visit to Nabbs Creek Crab Garden was an enjoyable one: a delicious crab dip, a couple of cold beers, and a jumbo crab cake. Life was good. I met the owners, learned the history of the restaurant, made new friends and promised to return. I did, only to find new owners and new crab cakes. Again I promised to return!

JANET'S PLACE CRAB PIZZA

🦀 *Did you know that pizza was made popular in the United States by soldiers who brought the idea back from Italy at the end of World War II? The Italians get the credit, but pizza is actually thought to have evolved from early Egyptian flat bread. By the way, don't be afraid to use more garlic than this recipe calls for!*

1   **pizza dough for 14 x 10-inch pan**
TOPPING
2   **avocados**
1   **tablespoon lemon juice**
4   **tablespoons butter**
2   **green onions, white part only**
1   **clove garlic, chopped**
½   **cup all-purpose flour**
1¼   **cups milk**
    salt and freshly ground black pepper
¼   **teaspoon cayenne pepper**
1   **pound crabmeat**
½   **cup shredded Swiss cheese**
    avocado and tomato slices

Preheat oven to 425°F. Roll out pizza dough and use to line a 14 x 10-inch jelly roll pan.

Halve avocados; remove pits. Scoop out flesh and chop coarsely. Place in a bowl with lemon juice and stir lightly to coat. Set aside. Melt the butter in a saucepan and add onion and garlic. Cook until translucent. Stir in flour and cook for 2 minutes. Stir in milk and bring mixture to a boil. Reduce heat and simmer for 2 minutes. Season to taste with salt and black pepper and cayenne pepper.

Remove pan from heat and stir in crabmeat, cheese, and chopped avocado. Spread over the dough and bake until crust is golden, about 20 minutes. Cool slightly before cutting into squares. Garnish with avocado and tomato slices.

Serves 6 to 8.

By the looks of the sign, someone may have been hurt while crabbing on this pier. So don't crab here. Colonial Beach, circa 1985.

226

CRABTOWN BAKED CRAB

🦀 *Here's an easy buffet dish for summer enter-taining. You can prepare it in the morning and the entire meal can be laid out on the buffet table while you circulate and enjoy the party. Just pop the Crabtown Crab into the oven at the last minute.*

4	tablespoons butter
1	shallot, chopped
½	cup sliced mushrooms
½	teaspoon tarragon vinegar
¼	cup sour cream at room temperature
¼	teaspoon grated nutmeg
	salt
8	ounces crabmeat
½	cup coarsely chopped cooked shrimp
1	egg, beaten
	grated Parmigiano-Reggiano cheese
	Italian seasoned breadcrumbs
	paprika

Melt 2½ tablespoons of the butter in a skillet over medium-high heat. Add shallot and sauté lightly. Stir in mushrooms and vinegar and cook for 2 minutes. Remove from heat and stir in sour cream, nutmeg, and salt to taste. Fold in crab-meat, shrimp and egg. Spoon into individual ramekins and sprinkle with Parmigiano-Reggiano cheese, breadcrumbs and paprika. Dot with remaining butter and broil just until golden.

Serves 4.

While visiting Hampton, Virginia, I spotted the Crabtown Fish Market. You guessed it—my car suddenly changed lanes and dropped me right at the front door. I didn't even ask it to! Is it magic?

227

CHESAPEAKE FARM CRAB WRAP-UPS

🦀 *Chili sauce is a spicy blend of tomatoes, chilies or chili powder, onions, green peppers, vinegar, sugar and spices. This ketchup-like sauce is used as a condiment, and its sweetness is what brings out the flavor of these crab wrap-ups.*

8	ounces crabmeat
½	cup shredded Monterey Jack cheese
½	cup shredded zucchini
¼	cup finely chopped celery
¼	cup finely chopped onion
3	tablespoons chili sauce
½	teaspoon salt
12	slices white sandwich bread
3	tablespoons melted butter
	Avocado Sauce (recipe follows)

Mix crabmeat, cheese, zucchini, celery, onion, chili sauce and salt. Roll each slice of bread to about 1/4-inch thickness. Spoon crabmeat mixture across the center of each slice; bring the sides of the bread up over the crabmeat mixture and secure with toothpicks. Place wrap-ups, seam-side down, in an unbuttered baking dish, brush with butter, and cook uncovered at 350°F until golden brown and hot, about 30 minutes. Serve with Avocado Sauce.

Serves 6.

AVOCADO SAUCE:

½	cup sour cream
1	small clove garlic, minced
½	teaspoon salt
1	medium tomato, chopped and drained
1	medium avocado, chopped

Heat sour cream and salt just until warm. Gently stir in garlic and tomato; heat for 1 minute. Remove from heat and gently stir in the avocado.

I spotted this crab sign outside the P.G.N. Crab House in Ocean City, Maryland. The result of this random stop? Another roll of film, another dozen steamed crabs, another delightful day.

JOHNSON'S STORE SEA TROUT STUFFED WITH CRAB

Sweet marjoram, usually simply called "marjoram," has small, oval, pale green leaves and a mild, sweet, oregano-like flavor. Its smell is captivating, and when I harvest a handful to use in this dish, I rub it into my beard so its fragrance can stay with me for a while.

¼   **cup fresh breadcrumbs**
8   **ounces crabmeat**
1   **tablespoon chopped fresh sweet marjoram**
1   **teaspoon salt**
½   **teaspoon pepper**
2   **tablespoons butter, melted**
4   **whole sea trout, 8 ounces each, cleaned, head and tail intact**
    additional sweet marjoram

In a bowl, combine breadcrumbs, crabmeat, sweet marjoram, salt, and pepper. Add butter and toss lightly to mix. Season cavity of the sea trout with salt and pepper. Loosely fill with crab stuffing and secure with toothpicks. Place trout flat on a steaming rack set over simmering water. Steam, covered, until fish is firm when pressed in center, about 10 minutes. Remove toothpicks and serve garnished with additional sweet marjoram.

Serves 4.

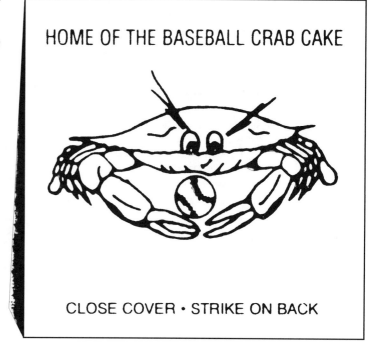

HOME OF THE BASEBALL CRAB CAKE

CLOSE COVER • STRIKE ON BACK

Roy's Kwik Korner at Crain Highway and Quarterfield Road in Glen Burnie, Maryland, is the home of the baseball crab cake. If you double that up with a bowl of crab soup, why you've touched all the bases!

229

FRESH SPINACH SALAD WITH WHARF DRESSING

🦀 *The best salad is a study in contrast and balance of textures, colors and flavors. Mix crunchy ingredients with those that are soft, tangy flavors with the mild or slightly sweet, and bright colors with the more muted. The results will be eye-pleasing, palate-teasing and downright delicious.*

½   **pound washed fresh spinach, finely shredded**
1   **small Bermuda onion, minced**
¼   **cup diced celery**
3   **hard-boiled eggs, sliced**
8   **ounces crabmeat**
    Wharf Dressing (recipe follows)

Toss the spinach, onion, celery and eggs together. Just before serving, add crabmeat and toss gently. Serve with Wharf Dressing.
    Serves 4.

WHARF DRESSING:
¾   **cup chili sauce**
1   **cup mayonnaise**
1   **tablespoon grated onion**
¼   **cup pickle relish**
1   **teaspoon lemon juice**
1   **teaspoon Worcestershire sauce, or to taste**
½   **teaspoon horseradish**

Combine ingredients and blend well.
Serves 4.

*S*howtimes for the Blues Brothers are 8 a.m. to noon and 5 p.m. to midnight snack.

INDEX

Index

Soups